SPEAKER'S TREASURY OF ANECDOTES
ABOUT THE FAMOUS

Books by James C. Humes

Speaker's Treasury of Anecdotes About the Famous

How to Get Invited to the White House

Roles Speakers Play

Podium Humor

Instant Eloquence

Speaker's Treasury of Anecdotes About the Famous

JAMES C. HUMES

HARPER & ROW, PUBLISHERS

NEW YORK, HAGERSTOWN, SAN FRANCISCO,
LONDON

FIRST EDITION

Designed by Sidney Feinberg

Library of Congress Cataloging in Publication Data

Humes, James C
  Speaker's treasury of anecdotes about the famous
James C. Humes.
  Includes index.
  1. Anecdotes. I. Title
PN4193.I5H84 1978   808.88′2   77–3754
ISBN 0–06–012008–0

---

78 79 80 10 9 8 7 6 5 4 3 2 1

To J. D. WILLIAMS
who first encouraged me to collect
stories, some of which were his own

CONTENTS

Acknowledgments

For assistance in research in the Library of Congress, I am deeply appreciative to A.R., F.P., and P.B.H.

For her reading, typing, and editing of my scrawled notes, I am, as always, grateful to S.L., who for ten years has been my loyal right hand.

PART I

How and Why to Use Anecdotes
in Speeches

What is history but the stories of the great? People make history come alive. They also make speeches come alive. In school I always enjoyed history, but it was not until I went to England in 1952 as an English-Speaking Union Exchange Scholar to a British public school that reading history became an obsession. That was because of Sir Winston Churchill. While in Britain that coronation year of 1953, we young American exchange students, like young "ambassadors," were invited to many functions to which ordinary tourists were not.

At one, which the Duke of Edinburgh attended, there was a galaxy of British cabinet officers and government officials. When the Prince asked me—I was then eighteen—what I hoped to do in life, I said, "To enter politics, sir." Whereupon Philip hailed Churchill, who was nearby, and while introducing us said, "He says he would like to go into government and politics."

Churchill looked at me and said, "Young man, study history, study history—in history lie all the secrets of statecraft." When I went back that night to my room at school, down came the photo of Ted Williams and up went one of Sir Winston Churchill out of the *Illustrated London News*. I have been a Churchill fanatic ever since. I have read all his books as well as biographies of him and I have played him on stage and television. During my life I have known many people active in politics who were first stirred by hero worship in a presidential campaign—Ike or Stevenson in 1952, J.F.K. in 1960, Goldwater in 1964, Gene McCarthy in 1968. Later on, after involvement in many political affairs and campaigns, one doesn't lose his heart so easily. Anyway, the candidate one works for often seems to pale beside the memory of one's first political hero.

Well, for me, that hero was Churchill. And even admitting my bias, I don't see other twentieth-century figures glowing with the splendor of that man. You see, when I met him he was already a legend like Caesar or Napoleon but he was alive. F.D.R., the other giant of World War II, had been dead for eight years, but Churchill had made a comeback to be elected prime minister once again.

As Churchill advised, I read history. I followed just one rule— I read only what I found enjoyable. The result was I bought as well as borrowed from libraries a lot of biographies—particularly anecdotal biographies. I never forced myself to finish a book. There was too much of that in school and college. An uncle of Oliver Wendell Holmes was told once by the future Justice, "If you can't remember the color of the heroine's eyes after the first seventy pages, don't bother to finish it."

Well, if by the first seventy pages, the biographer is still sketching the background and childhood of the subject, I put down the book.

Once when I was in college, a history professor went to the library to check out a few books on early nineteenth-century British history. Out of the fifteen books he checked out, my name was on fourteen of the library cards. Word spread that I had read more books than any of the faculty. Of course, I had read only a few of them—ten or more I immediately returned when they didn't catch my interest.

Another thing I learned from Churchill's writings of his early life was not only to read what you enjoy but to file away those ideas, phrases, or anecdotes in your reading that strike a responsive chord. At home I now have black looseleaf notebooks that piled up together would reach the ceiling. It was these notebooks that landed me my job as a White House speech writer.

In 1968 Richard Nixon, whom I knew while I was in law school, was aware of my extensive collection and occasionally would have someone call me for a quotation or an inspirational vignette from history. When Nixon was elected, he called me to Washington to work as one of his speech writers even though my profession was not journalism but law. Bill Safire in his book *Before the Fall* quotes a presidential memorandum to the staff that said, "Why can't the rest of you come up with stories like Jamie Humes?"

What Richard Nixon liked in my anecdotes was not only their historical significance but also their ease of assimilation. Presidents Nixon and Ford, unlike Lyndon Johnson, did not like to read their speeches. For their utterances on ceremonial occasions in the Rose Garden, they preferred to talk without a text. A story out of history helps you to do that, for you do not have to remember a series of phrased paragraphs but just a picture—and one or two sentences.

One story that Richard Nixon used before a national prayer breakfast involved a White House meeting of Abraham Lincoln with a group of Methodist clergy. The delegation's leader said he was confident that the cause of the Union would prevail because God was on their side. Lincoln replied that the question was not whether God was on our side but whether we were on *His* side. Nixon used the story to talk about the healthy need to guard against piousness by honest self-examination. Nixon called such stories "parables"—talks which bore a message. Actually I got the idea of turning such historical vignettes into speech fodder from Ted Sorensen. Sorensen, the chief wordsmith for John Kennedy, had a file of them on hand for use in short informal remarks.

You will see in the hundreds of speeches by John Kennedy the use of a closing anecdote to leave the audience inspired. In one he closes with Lincoln's short farewell to his friends at a Springfield railroad platform. For another he quotes Benjamin Franklin at the Constitutional Convention looking at the president's chair which had carved on its back a sun low on the horizon ("For a time I thought it was a setting sun, but now I know it's a rising sun—a new day for America and a new dawn for freedom"). In still another Kennedy describes Louis Brandeis being interrogated by a hostile congressional committee, which was questioning the future Supreme Court Justice's credentials in his appearance testifying about public land frauds. (When asked whom he represented,

Brandeis replied, "I represent the people—the public is my client"). In my book *Instant Eloquence* (Harper & Row, 1973) I devote a whole chapter to such stories—I call them "Soul-Shakers." They are memorable not only for the beauty of what was said but where and how the words came about. The scene is often as important as the statement.

On a national talk show I was asked recently what comprised great oratory. I replied that most people named one of three speeches as the most poignant in their lifetime: J.F.K.'s inaugural address in 1961: "Ask not what your country can do for you, but rather what you can do for your country"; Martin Luther King's "I have a dream" speech before the steps of the Lincoln Memorial at the end of the civil rights march in the summer of 1963; or General Douglas MacArthur's farewell remarks to the joint houses of Congress following his dismissal by President Truman—"Old soldiers never die, they just fade away."

What made these remarks etch themselves forever in the memories of the listeners was the occasion as much as the oratory —a young president starting out, an embattled civil rights crusader culminating the largest demonstration ever seen in American history, or a heroic general closing out his long military career on an issue of principle.

What engages the mind in each of these famous instances is the dramatic circumstances—a famous man at a critical moment in history. As in the painting I once saw of Patrick Henry speaking at a Richmond Episcopal church to fellow Virginia convention delegates. The engraved plaque underneath read: PATRICK HENRY: "Give me liberty or give me death," March 23, 1775.

The Chinese said that a picture is worth a thousand words. The tales I include in this book are in a sense both—they are word pictures.

It is interesting that Richard Nixon chose to call these word pictures out of history "parables." The greatest exponent of parabolic teaching was Jesus Christ. The stories he told have lived for almost two thousand years. Think of just a few of them—the prodigal son, the good Samaritan, the Pharisee and the publican, the rich man and Lazarus. The stories Jesus told were easily remembered by his followers. Compare Paul with Christ. Paul was a theologian, but Christ was a teacher. Paul in his letters wrote doctrine but Christ told stories. It is the storyteller who is the real teacher.

President Ford in a White House ceremony in 1976 honored a black woman teacher from North Carolina. The President asked her, "What subjects do you teach?" The seventh-grade teacher replied, "I don't teach subjects. I teach children."

The same is true of public speaking. Pedants discourse on subjects, but the good speaker like the good teacher gives himself. Think back to the teachers you most remember from school—they did not present objective analysis, but conveyed their enthusiasm by being subjective, relating their own involvement and their own experiences. I had a teacher of ancient history who spoke of Pericles, Demosthenes, and Plato as if they were his contemporaries. We half believed it since he was well over eighty. He made history come alive by talking of Pericles's mistress and Alcibiades's double-agent activities. History is people and so are current events.

Recently a friend of mine of Italian ancestry was asked to speak to the Sons of Italy. Since he was about to announce his candidacy for governor of his state, he wanted to win their support. I told him to forget about the current legislative session and speak from his heart about their common heritage and hopes. "Go to Ellis Island next weekend," I told him. "Sail around the island—picture what your grandfather felt the first time he saw the Statue of Liberty. Talk to your father—he'll tell you what your grandfather felt on that momentous day." He wrote his speech using this approach and it brought tears to many of the listeners.

Although I gave this advice before *Roots* was shown on television, Alex Haley's book does satisfy the yearning of people to see history unfold through personal experience. Genealogist friends of mine report that they have been deluged with requests for help in obtaining family histories. The history of every American, except the Indian, is that of an immigrant who came to the New World with a dream for a better future for his children.

Probably the most gifted White House speech writer a recent President ever used was the poet and dramatist Archibald MacLeish. MacLeish, who wrote for F.D.R., penned some of the most beautiful words about the American mission ("There are those, I know, who will reply that the liberation of humanity, the freedom of man and mind is nothing but a dream. They are right. It is the American dream").

MacLeish, whose father had emigrated from Scotland, was once asked how he came to understand and express the meaning of the American Revolution. He replied that his maternal grandfather was a young minister at the time of the Civil War. The young clergyman had the idea of interviewing the living survivors of the Revolutionary War and having Mathew Brady photograph them. One of the veterans over a hundred years old told MacLeish's grandfather of his meeting George Washington after the concluding victory over the British at Yorktown. "Boy," said the commander-in-chief to the young drummer, "go out and buy thirteen candles and light them tonight for the new thirteen independent states."

Think of our glorious American history telescoped in a family anecdote.

I remember in my own childhood being introduced at a family gathering to a cousin who remembered great-great-grandmother Mary Humes, a widow of a Revolutionary War soldier. We all have such stories in our family history—personal anecdotes or experiences that are threads in the tapestry of our rich American heritage.

Today history has become a boring subject for children because we have ceased to make it exciting. We no longer excite them about the courage of a Washington or the idealism of a Lincoln. Yet their reaction might be different if we told how Washington decided as a thirteen-year-old boy to enter military service when he first saw his older half-brother who had returned home from fighting on the Spanish Main as a blue-uniformed officer in the British Navy. (Mount Vernon was named by Lawrence Washington after the admiral under whom he served in that campaign.) Or we can describe Lincoln's revulsion when he saw, as a young man in downstate Illinois, blacks his own age being auctioned off into slavery.

I often volunteer to speak to first-graders on subjects that introduce them to the great men of history. One is the history of the Teddy Bear. I tell how it was named after Theodore Roosevelt, who had once rescued a bear cub from being killed. Then I relate how Winnie the Pooh owes his name to "Winnie" Churchill. In my English school days I had the room that was once occupied by Christopher Robin Milne, son of the famous children's author A. A. Milne. Because of meeting him and his famous ursine companion, I am able to instill in my very young audience a desire to hear more about Teddy Roosevelt and Winston Churchill.

Another story I tell primary-school children is "mice day." I have taken an episode of my own family history as the basis of the story. One of my ancestors, Israel Cole, gave a three-hundred-pound Cheshire cheese to Andrew Jackson as an inaugural present in 1829. In the free-for-all that followed Jackson's opening the White House to all his followers, the cheese was ground down into the floor. So I make the day the mice's national holiday with a story about the original White House mice.

Not long ago a candidate for high public office came to me for speech advice. The young man, scion of an established Eastern family long active in public affairs, faced a tough fight. I told him, "Look, you come off as earnest, honest, and dedicated but people want to know how you feel. They don't think WASPs understand things the way they see them. They look at you, a handsome product from the best boarding school and college, and wonder if you know—if you have experienced the basic problems of life. Tell them in your speeches what you have told me over the dinner table. Give them your feelings, not just the facts."

I asked the candidate to think over all the personal tragedies in his life, the disappointments, the frustrated hopes, the moments of defeat—the death of loved ones, "the times you were turned down for a job or a promotion. Then come back to me and we'll see how you can use those experiences to explain your various positions on certain issues or proposals."

In *Alice Through the Looking Glass* the King says, "The honor of the moment—I shall never forget." "You will, though," the Queen said, "if you don't make a memorandum of it." So take time out to make a memo to yourself of all the poignant moments in your life—what your father said to you before you went to college or when you got your first car. Or maybe, it was the first death of one of your family or the time you were fired through a misunderstanding. See how each of these stories can tell a point for use in a speech.

The eighteenth-century English portraitist Sir Joshua Reynolds was once asked by his host why he did not paint pictures of the town where he was visiting. Replied Sir Joshua, "The human face is my landscape."

Audiences react to stories not statistics. Give them experiences not abstractions. In December 1976, I was asked as a White House speech writer to speak to the Republican Governors Conference in Washington. "Too long," I told the governors and their staffs, "the Republican Party has been seen as being more interested in profits than people. I support the concepts of free enterprise, individual initiative, and fiscal stability, but we must not confuse the means with the end. These principles are abstractions that audiences can't feel or touch. Try for once not to use those catch phrases in a speech. Instead talk about the 'family,' the 'community,' or the 'neighborhood.' People won't fight just to preserve their bosses' profits but they will fight if problems are presented in terms of the future of their children, or the threat to their neighborhood or the community. The cause of a balanced budget means nothing unless you say how the future of their children and their children's children is being mortgaged."

You will recall in the first presidential debate between Ford and Carter, the closings came after a sustained delay because of technical difficulties with the TV transmission. Although it was generally conceded that Ford edged the Georgia Governor in the question and answer, many thought that Carter's sum-up was more effective. The Georgian was more personal than political, while the incumbent President ended with standard Republican clichés about free enterprise and balanced budgets.

I had urged the President to speak from his heart and say why he wanted to continue in the job. The closing I recommended, which was rejected, went like this:

> I did not seek to be President but when a constitutional crisis developed, I accepted my responsibility. I did not seek to be Vice President but when the Chief Executive with the almost unanimous consent of Congress turned to me, I accepted the responsibility.
>
> Later I became President in one of the most difficult periods in our nation's history. I tried to do my level best. I don't say that I completely succeeded, but I think you will agree that times today seem brighter than they were then. All of you remember the tall ships and wagon trains of last July Fourth. Millions of people from San Francisco to New York, without a single riot or incident, celebrated their heritage. They rang bells, sang in churches and danced in the streets. More than any mission to the Moon or Mars, this spontaneous outpouring of affection proved to the world that America had regained her role as the guardian of democratic hopes and dreams. I don't claim to have done this. You the American people, by reaching back into your own roots, rekindled our pride. No President, by signing a paper or enacting a bill, can lift the spirit of the nation. He can only hope by setting the right tone and charting a true course that he helped restore the faith and renew confidence.
>
> This I tried to do. I tried to heal the wounds of War and Watergate —I tried to check inflation and revive a depressed economy. I know I haven't completely succeeded—I know I've made my share of mistakes but I ask you to let me finish the job.
>
> Years ago my good friend General Eisenhower bought a farm in Gettysburg. At the recording of the deed in the courthouse, a clerk asked him, "General, why when you live in New York as President of Columbia University, do you want this land in Pennsylvania?" And General Eisenhower replied, "I want once in my life to take a piece of land and return it to God better than I found it."
>
> With God's help will you join me in making our land a brighter land for our children and our children's children.

In my view, the closing story capped all the feelings the President should have conveyed and would have struck a responsive chord in all of us parents who have tried to do our own task of building a home and future for our children.

Anecdotes like the one about Eisenhower can reach the heart

by striking the right chord. When in my twenties I ran for the Pennsylvania legislature, I opposed in the Republican primary an incumbent respected by party regulars. Because primaries are often the most bitter of political fights, I wanted to take care that I didn't permanently alienate the old guard whose support I would need in the autumn. I would close my appeals to Republican groups with this story from the Bible:

> Finally, I want to say that more important than winning is earning your trust. I hope this contest has strengthened our party and I pray that, win or lose, I can say at the end of this campaign as the Apostle Paul said just before his death in the final message he sent from his Roman jail to his adopted son Timothy, "I have fought a good fight, I have finished the race, I have kept the faith."

Anecdotes are also useful for opening short presentations or talks. Two I have found helpful are ones involving two sages—one ancient and the other recent—Buddha and Oliver Wendell Holmes.

In his early career Buddha was in the service of a prince. A palace aide relayed to Buddha an inquiry from his master. The prince wanted to know the single most important advice he could give about administration. Buddha told the servant, "Tell him to begin by defining the nature of the problem."

Late in Holmes's career, the great Supreme Court Justice found himself on a train. The jurist, then in his late eighties, was approached by the conductor for his ticket. When Holmes could not locate it, the conductor said to him, "Never mind, Mr. Justice. "I know I have it," said Holmes. "But what I want to know is where in the world I am supposed to be going."

As soon as you mention a great name, people's interest perks up. The audience's interest is whetted and their curiosity pricked. When *Life* magazine failed, the Luce group started *People* because surveys told them that gossip about the famous was the single greatest factor in expanding readership these days. Television, with shows like Johnny Carson, Dinah Shore, and Mike Douglas, has proved that "celebrities" are entertainment's biggest business. Mediocre movies become box-office smashes just because

Robert Redford or Paul Newman stars in them. Big newspapers, threatened by television's increasing hold on advertising, feature gossip columns. Such columns, which were once restricted to tidbits on Hollywood by Louella Parsons and Hedda Hopper, have now moved to the editorial pages. Even the *New York Times* has a section which reports items about nationally known figures. The best-read parts of the Sunday supplements have now become answers to questions about the private lives of senators and authors as well as actors and swingers. The life of America is fueled by gossip. Eavesdrop on any lunch in New York, Washington, or Los Angeles and you will hear names dropped between each sip or bite. Washington is now called by some "Hollywood East" because reputations are made or maintained by their accessibility to the famous. If glamor is the appeal in Hollywood, it is power in our nation's capital.

Once at the Sans Souci, the restaurant that is catty-corner to the White House, I was discussing with its famous maître d' Paul de Lisle the secret of his success. "Paul," I said, "other restaurants have good French food, yet yours is the place to be seen in." "Monsieur Humes, Washington is ze city of ze powerful—it is power, zen ze access to power, and zen ze illusion of ze access to power."

In 1940 an alderman related to New York Democratic boss Ed Flynn his fears about the fall election. Flynn looked out his window at the New York harbor and said, "Hymie, do you see the big ocean liner that is coming into port?" "Yes," said Hymie. "You have seen how, when it comes in, it brings in on its trail all kinds of riffraff and debris?" "Yes," said Hymie, "but what does it have to do with my election?" "Well, President Franklin Roosevelt runs this year, and he is going to carry into office with him all kinds of people like you."

In speeches, too, the name of the great and famous generates its kind of power. Let the names Roosevelt and Holmes run interference for you. The very mention of a well-known name stirs the audience's interest. They particularly like to hear how the powerful react to the simple problems of life we all have.

Over the years I have kept notes on the habits of various public personalities I have known. Perle Mesta, the Washington hostess, told me the secret of her successful parties was saying "at last" as each guest arrived and "so soon" to each one as they left.

When I visited the late Lord Avon (Anthony Eden) in England in 1971, the one-time British Prime Minister indicated that he did most of his serious thinking while gardening. "At my desk I always felt overwhelmed by the details of administration but in the garden I seemed to view things with clearer vision."

Bill Scranton, former U.S. Ambassador to the United Nations, said that the most important words in his meetings and talks with other delegates was "you," "your people," or "your nation." It echoed something the late President Eisenhower told me about MacArthur. "Mac," he said, "was a great orator but he was not so great in selling on a one-to-one relationship. His problem was that he seemed addicted to the vertical pronoun."

After my encounters with the great I record in my diary their views on even the most trivial matters—what they like to eat, their favorite films, the books that most influenced them. I know that somehow it is all material that I will find helpful in my books and lectures. You can do the same. Always take a notepad with you when you go to a lecture or attend church. If you like a certain anecdote or quotation, the chances are others will too. So write it down for future reference.

My daughter Rachel was once asked in the first grade what her father did for a living. She said I was a "paster." No doubt, she assumed that because she saw me so much in our library pasting, clipping, and filing away the tidbits I collected in my day's reading and travels into my huge notebook file. It is out of this file that I have gleaned many of the stories in this book. Abraham Lincoln once said, "I am only a retailer—I collect stories I have heard other people tell." Most of the famous lecturers do likewise. They know that the secret of a good talk is to make it entertaining whether it be a political speech, a classroom lecture, or even a good night's conversation.

Felix Frankfurter, the late Supreme Court Justice, was once dawdling in a taxi cab before a home he was about to visit. The driver, puzzled by the delay, asked, "Is this the right address?" "Yes," said Frankfurter. "I'm just going over in my mind some of the stories I can tell tonight at the dinner table."

The next time before you go out, whether it's to be as a speaker or a dinner companion, try going over some of the stories in this book. You'll be the hit of the evening.

PART II

Nearly 600 Anecdotes About

Famous People

Abuse—*Response*

In regard to the remarks of that party, let me tell you of an incident between Henry Clay and John Randolph. The cantankerous Congressman John Randolph of Virginia was walking down a narrow street in early, muddy Washington when Henry Clay, his arch-political foe, was coming the other way. Said the irascible Randolph, "I never give way to a scoundrel." "I do," replied Clay, as he yielded the right of way to Randolph.

Similarly, I am not going to get involved with the gentleman in my case. Let him go his own peculiar way . . .

Accident—*Discovery*

At the Savoy in London before World War I, when César Ritz was maître d'hôtel and Escoffier was chef, Nellie Melba, the celebrated prima donna from Australia, while staying at the hotel was dieting strenuously, living largely on toast. It chanced one day, while the master was preoccupied, that an underling prepared the great lady's toast. It was bungled and was served to her in a thin dried-up state resembling parchment. Ritz beheld with horror his celebrated guest crunching this aborted toast, and hastened over to apologize. Before he could utter a word Madame Melba burst out joyfully, "César, how clever of Escoffier. I have never eaten such lovely toast." Thereafter it was called Melba Toast.

Well, sometimes it is through accident, that we make our most brilliant discoveries . . .

Achievement—*Audience*

Dr. Johnson and his friend Boswell were at Drury Lane Theatre together watching the great actor Garrick. Boswell said to Johnson, "Garrick is not himself tonight," and the great man replied, "No."

All at once Garrick commenced to act superbly, and Boswell remarked, "Do you notice how he has changed and changed for the better?" "Yes," said the old sage, "and did you notice at what point he changed? He took a higher style when Edmund Burke came into the theater."

All of us tend to do our best when we know the right people are going to be watching . . .

Achievement—*Record*

When Charles M. Schwab had not yet become a great industrialist in his own right, he worked for Andrew Carnegie. The little Scotsman taught him the hard lesson of the commercial world, that one day's laurels are of little use on the next. "All records broken yesterday," Schwab once wired to his chief. In reply to which Carnegie telegraphed, "But what have you done today?"

Similarly, we cannot rest on yesterday's laurels . . .

Action—*Inaction*

Once when the Yankees were playing the Cleveland Indians Yankee hitter Moose Skowron whacked the ball down the right-field line, and Rocky Colavito made a great try for it. He took a long sitting slide, but just missed the ball. As luck would have it, he landed on the ball and couldn't find it. Everyone in the park—except Rocky—knew he was sitting on it.

In front of the Indian dugout, screaming like a lunatic, was Manager Joe Gordon. "For heaven's sake," he kept yelling, "somebody tell him to get off the ball before he hatches it."

And it's about time we begin to pick up the ball and . . .

It is about time we start to work. Even the great patience of Abraham Lincoln once was exhausted by his reluctant generals. When Joe Hooker replaced Burnside as commander of the Army of the Potomac, Hooker, in order to create the impression of immense and vigorous activity, reported his movements in a dispatch headed HEADQUARTERS IN THE SADDLE. "The trouble with Hooker," the unimpressed Lincoln remarked, "is that he's got his headquarters where his hindquarters ought to be."

Similarly, we have to get off our behinds . . .

Adjournment—*Late*

After giving a speech one night, Chauncey M. Depew was surrounded by a group of female enthusiasts. "Oh, Mr. Depew!" exclaimed one of the ladies. "You said in your speech that sleep was the most beautiful thing in the world. I thought you would say a woman was." "Well," said Depew, thoughtfully, "next to a beautiful woman, sleep is!"

Well, whoever our partners are, I think it is getting to be the time of the evening when we should adjourn . . .

Advantage—*Handicap*

Former Pirate slugger Ralph Kiner was telling his broadcasting buddy, Lindsey Nelson, about his wife, the former tennis star Nancy Chaffee. "When I married Nancy, I vowed I'd beat her at tennis someday. After six months, she beat me 6–2. After a year, she beat me 6–4. After we were married a year and a half, I pushed her to 7–5. Then it happened—she had a bad day and I had a good one, and I beat her 17–15." "Good for you, Ralph," exclaimed Lindsey. "Was she sick?" "Of course not!" Kiner snapped indignantly. "Well, she was eight months pregnant."

Adversary—*Competitor*

Frederick II, King of Prussia, during a huge court dinner spied on the other side of the table General Landhohn, a French soldier who had been a gallant adversary in former battles. "Pray, sir," said Frederick, "take a place at my side. I have learned it is best not to have you opposite me."

And, similarly, I'm glad to have next to me, and not opposite me tonight . . .

Advice— *Value*

I was asked tonight to give my comments on some of the current questions. Now while I am a lawyer and acting in the role of adviser, I guess I don't rate the treatment super-lawyer Clark Clifford had in Washington. The story is told of his being called by a corporation president who explained a difficult problem. Clifford told him not to do anything or say anything. Then he sent a bill for $10,000. A few days later the executive called back and remarked, "Clark, first, this bill is way out of line, and second, why should I keep quiet anyway?" "Because I told you so," said Clifford as he hung up the phone and then proceeded to bill the client for another $5,000.

Age—*Ability*

I'm beginning to feel the same way the seventy-year-old pianist Mischa Elman did in 1962 when he was preparing to depart from the United States for a European concert tour and complained: "When I made my debut as a twelve-year-old in Berlin, people used to say, 'Isn't he wonderful for his age?' Now they're beginning to say the same thing again."

Age—*Active*

When the poet Henry Wadsworth Longfellow was well along in years his hair was white as snow, but his cheeks were as red as a rose. An admirer asked him how he was able to keep so vigorous and yet have time to write so beautifully. Pointing to a blossoming apple tree, the poet said, "That tree is very old, but I never saw prettier blossoms on it than those which it now bears. That tree grows new wood each year. Like that apple tree, I try to grow a little new wood each year."

Longfellow knew the secret of remaining young was developing new interests . . .

Age—*Birthday*

I thank you for coming to my birthday celebration. I hope some of you will return next year. Of course, that is subject to some contingency. I remember when Sir Winston Churchill greeted reporters in his yard on his eighty-seventh birthday. Said one young eager journalist, "I hope to again wish you well on your one hundredth birthday." The "Old Man" eyed the young newsman sternly and remarked "I expect you might do it—you look healthy enough."

Age—*Comparison*

When Third Baseman George Kell broke in with the Athletics, Bobo Newsom was in the twilight of his pitching career. In a tight game one afternoon, the Tigers had a man on first and one out. With every pitch by Newsom, Kell would charge in from third base for a bunt. Finally, with the count three and one, Bobo called for time and motioned Kell to the mound. "What are you trying to do to me?" he growled. "What do you mean?" Kell stammered. "I'm supposed to break down the line on your pitch, aren't I?" "Yeah," snapped Newsom, "but you're getting to the plate faster than my fast ball. You're making me look bad."

And, similarly, some of these young kids in the organization are making me look bad . . .

Age—*Conditions*

Even in his last years Winston Churchill liked to drop in at the House of Commons from time to time. One day when he was helped down the aisle to his seat by two aides, a couple of young M.P.s nearby started murmuring. "You know, I don't think he should come in any more," said one. "He's getting so dottery." The other whispered, "Yes, and they say he's even getting a bit soft in the upper story." Churchill slowly turned in his seat and rasped, "They also say that he's getting hard of hearing."

Well, gentlemen, I may be old but I'm still hearing things and some of the things I don't like . . .

Age—*Discretion*

Mary Garden, the magnificent Metropolitan Opera soprano of the 1920s, had a figure to match her talent. Once seeing her in a gown with very pronounced décolletage, the honorable Chauncey Depew in admiration asked her what kept her dress up. She replied, "Two things: your age and my discretion."

But in this case, it is *my* age as well *my* discretion that will make me refrain from telling you all that went on in those days . . .

Age—*Health*

When questions are asked about my health, I think of the words of John Quincy Adams. Once Daniel Webster ran into him and asked him how he was feeling. Adams drew a deep sigh and said, "I inhabit a weak, frail, decayed tenement, battered by the winds, and broken in upon by the storms, and from all I can learn, the landlord does not intend to repair."

Age—*Interests*

Thomas Edison, the inventor, knew the secret of youth. He was still inventing in his eighth decade. In the 1920s Henry Ford and Thomas Edison visited the California home of their mutual friend Luther Burbank. Burbank kept a guest book where his visitors would sign in. Beside the name and address spaces was a space marked "interests." Ford watched Edison write in that place "everything."

Age—*Lady*

It is always a pleasure to follow a lady on the rostrum. I recall what "Uncle Joe" Cannon said some years ago during a lengthy debate with a lady member of the House. "Uncle Joe," then in his eighties, rose and asked, "Will the lady yield?" When she continued to hold the floor, he asked again, "Will the distinguished lady please yield?" Finally she replied with a smile, "The lady will be delighted to yield, to the gentleman from Illinois." The aged Cannon then replied, "My God! Now that she has yielded, what can I do about it?"

Well, I guess I can say you have yielded me some sort of opportunity in letting me speak today . . .

Age—*Retirement*

When Daniel Webster, the great American lawyer, was on his last sickbed, he was visited by a friend who said to him, "Well, cheer up, Senator, I believe that your constitution will pull you through." "Not at all," said Webster, "my constitution was gone long ago, and I am living on my by-laws now."

Well, I'm not even living on my by-laws—perhaps on my in-laws . . .

⇌

For many years Harry Hershfield had always phoned Bernard Baruch on his birthday no matter where he was in the world— Europe, Israel—to wish him well. On Baruch's ninety-fifth birthday, Hershfield phoned him. During the course of the conversation, he asked, "Bernie, do you think there's as much love in the world today as there was years back?" "Yes," was the reply, "but there's another bunch doing it!"

I think it is time for another generation to assume responsibility —it is their turn to meet the problems and bear the criticism.

⇌

On March 8, 1931, on the occasion of his ninetieth birthday, Justice Oliver Wendell Holmes consented to deliver a radio talk. At the close, he said, "I end with a line from a Latin poet who uttered the message more than fifteen hundred years ago: 'Death plucks my ear and says, "Hurry, I am coming." ' "

⇌

Once a newspaper correspondent visited former President Coolidge at Northampton, Massachusetts. As he watched the automobiles passing by his home he remarked, "It must make you proud to see all these people coming by here, merely to look at you sitting on the porch. It shows that although you are an ex-President you are not forgotten. Just look at the number of those cars." "Not as many as yesterday," replied Mr. Coolidge. "There were 163 of them."

Well, I, too, find that fame is fleeting . . .

⸗

Legally I may be too old but physically and mentally I am not. I recall the time a lawyer from Alabama named Edmund Pettus went to Senator John Tyler Morgan and inquired about a federal judicial vacancy in his home state. The Senator, an old friend, was sympathetic, and in good spirits Mr. Pettus went to see the other Alabama Senator, James Pugh.

Senator Pugh told him, "Look, Ed, you are too old. I'm doing you a favor by telling you straight to quit—quit thinking about it. You've got no chance."

"So, Jim," said Pettus, "you think I'm too damned old to be a federal judge, do you? Well, Jim, I may be too old to be a judge but I'm not too old to be a United States Senator."

And he walked out of the Senator's office and went home to Alabama, ran against Pugh, and was elected.

⸗

I have always agreed with Austen Chamberlain's views on longevity. At a birthday party the British statesman was asked his secret of perpetual youth. He smiled and said, "Never walk if you can drive; and of two cigars always choose the longest and strongest."

⸗

On her eightieth birthday Helen Keller was asked, "How do you hope to approach old age?" Characteristically, she gave this classic reply: "One should never count the years—one should instead count his interests—I have kept young trying never to lose my childhood sense of wonderment. I am glad I still have a vivid curiosity about the world I live in."

And so I think I'm still as young as my interests and one of my interests is . . .

≡

During his last illness a number of Pennsylvania politicians called upon Thaddeus Stevens to pay their respects and in the course of the conversation one of them remarked on his appearance. "Oh, gentlemen," he said, "it is not my appearance that I am concerned about just now, but my disappearance."

Well, I am not going to completely disappear from the scene . . .

≡

I am at the age where we constantly muse about our mortality. One of the philosophic comments I remember is that of the publisher Lord Beaverbrook. Shortly before his death in London, he remarked at a dinner, "It is time for me to become an apprentice once more. I am not certain in which direction but somewhere, sometime soon."

Age—*Youth*

I recall the 1968 baseball season which produced only one .300 hitter in the American League. He was Carl Yastrzemski of the Boston Red Sox, who retained his batting title with a mark of only .301—the lowest batting average ever achieved by a major-league champion. When the old-time American League batting champion George Sisler was asked what he thought his batting average would be among the current crop of American League hitters, the Hall of Famer who twice had hit over .400 and wound up with a sixteen-year lifetime batting average of .340 said modestly, "Oh, I guess I would do as well as Yastrzemski did, and hit about .300!" "What, only .300?" asked one of his audience. "Don't forget, young man," said the old-timer, "come March, I'll be seventy-five years old."

But, seriously, I don't think, even with the advantages of youth, I could do as well . . .

≡

One night in the Lambs Club bar, actor David Wayne told a ribald story that drew a laugh from everybody but eighty-year-old Harry Hershfield. Wayne said, "What's the matter, Harry—can't you remember when you went out with girls?" Said veteran Hershfield, "Sure, I can remember when I went out with girls—but I can't remember what for."

But unfortunately for me, I can still remember what for—and that's worse . . .

Agreement—*Expert*

I find myself in agreement with the proposition if a little uncertain on the general details of execution. In that way I am not unlike George Washington, who as a member of Virginia's House of Burgesses in 1775 met secretly to discuss the worsening situation with Britain. At Williamsburg's Raleigh Tavern the dissident colonials talked strategy. Young Tom Jefferson said, "As for me, there is no country in the world I would rather be dependent on than Britain, but if the Tory government continues to deny us our rights, I would move body and soul to sink that island to the bottom of the Atlantic Ocean."

Colonel Washington replied, "The sentiments of Mr. Jefferson are also mine. It is the time to move for independence. But as a military man, I must say as to Mr. Jefferson's specific plan of routing the British, I will leave that to the naval experts."

And so while I generally approve of the project, I would like to consult . . .

Amateurs—*Professional*

This is a situation where we shouldn't trust amateur advice. We need the best professional appraisal no matter what the cost. It is the same advice Talleyrand once gave to Louis XVIII. King Louis was reading a tentative budget to Talleyrand, who was head of the provisional government. "Your Majesty, I note an omission," commented Talleyrand.

"Well?"

"Payment of the deputies."

"I think they should perform their duties without any payment; it should be an honorary position," said Louis.

"Without any payment?" cried Talleyrand. "Without any payment? Your Majesty, that would cost us much too much!"

Ambition—*Retirement*

General U. S. Grant responded to the New York *Herald*'s editorial suggesting him for the presidency with this remark to the press: "I aspire only to one political office. When this war is over, the only office I'd run for is Mayor of Galena, my home town in Illinois, where I'd like to have the sidewalk fixed up between my house and the depot."

And, similarly, if I could have the road fixed up to the golf course . . .

Amendment—*Editing*

When the Continental Congress debated the content and wording of the final draft of the Declaration of Independence on July 2-3, 1776, cutting out passages and rewriting others, Franklin comforted Jefferson, whose pride of authorship was hurt, by telling him a characteristic story. This tale concerned a hat maker who decided to put a sign in front of his shop that showed a picture of a hat and read "John Thompson, Hatter, makes and sells hats for ready money." One friend said the word "Hatter" was not needed; another said "makes and" was unnecessary; and a third friend said that the sign would be simpler if it just said "John Thompson sells hats." Finally, a fourth friend reminded him that people seeing the picture of the hat on the sign would not expect him to give hats away, so that really all he needed on the sign was his name and the picture of the hat.

As a printer Ben Franklin understood the demands for economy of space, and as a political writer Jefferson came to understand the need for editing. As for me, I can go along with the proposed changes . . .

America—*Patriotism*

On July 4, 1876, crowds gathered in Concord, Massachusetts, to hear Ralph Waldo Emerson's Centennial address. Senator Rufus Choate, a tight-buttoned lawyer who filled Daniel Webster's unexpired term in the 1840s, was unmoved by the cadences of Emerson's oratory. Afterward he made light fun of it, calling it full of the "glittering and sounding generalities that make up the Declaration of Independence." On hearing this the immigrant Carl Schurz, who had come over from Germany believing in the spirit of revolutionary freedom expressed in Jefferson's Declaration, took offense. " 'Glittering generalities'?" he said. "Those are blazing ubiquities!"

Indeed, the ideals of the Declaration of Independence continue to blaze the sky as torches of freedom not only here but everywhere in the world . . .

Appeasement—*Courage*

British Foreign Secretary Sir Alec Douglas-Home was praised in 1972 for expelling over one hundred Soviet spies who were using a diplomatic cover. He was lauded for his courage in doing what few Western leaders have dared to. Yet Sir Alec was a modest man. Referring to his recovery from spinal tuberculosis in 1942, he said, "I am one of the few politicians who can actually and truly say he has a steel backbone inserted in his spine."

Well, today in dealing with the Soviets, we need more statesmen with steel in their spines . . .

Approach—*Sensitivity*

Once when Arturo Toscanini was rehearsing Debussy's *La Mer*, he wanted to achieve a highly sublime effect in one spot. At a loss for words to describe what he wanted to do, he took from his breast pocket a large white silk handkerchief. He threw it high into the air, and every man in the orchestra was hypnotized as it floated softly, sensuously to the floor. "There," the Maestro smiled happily, "play it like that."

Now, although I don't have a silk handkerchief with which to demonstrate, it is just this sensitive, delicate approach we should adopt . . .

Architect—*Mistake*
One of the most sensational trials in American history occurred when millionaire Harry Thaw shot architect Sanford White in a quarrel over the lovely Evelyn Nesbit. Thaw was given ten years in Sing Sing Prison. Shortly after he was released, he attended the grand opening of the Roxy Theater in New York. As he gazed in horror at the Hollywood-Byzantine splendor of the lobby, he gasped, "My God, I shot the wrong architect!"

Well, fortunately we didn't choose the wrong architect for our new . . .

Architect—*Unique*
When the onion-domed masterpiece St. Basil's was completed in Moscow's Red Square, Ivan the Terrible invited its three major architects to participate in the dedicatory mass. Then with a knife he cut out their eyes so that they would not be tempted to duplicate the structure.

Well, our architects, engineers, and builders don't have to worry, it would be impossible now to duplicate this effort . . .

Argument—*Debate*
The speech we just heard reminds me of Abraham Lincoln's characterization of Stephen Douglas at the time of their Senate campaign debates in Illinois. "When I was a boy," said Lincoln, "I spent considerable time along the Sangamon River. An old steamboat plied on the river, the boiler of which was so small that when they blew the whistle, there wasn't enough steam to turn the paddle wheel. When the paddle wheel went around, they couldn't blow the whistle. My friend Douglas," said Lincoln, "reminds me of that old steamboat, for it is evident that when he talks he can't think, and when he thinks he can't talk."

Now, similarly, our friend on the opposing side wasn't thinking when he said . . .

Argument—*Logic*

The logic of my opponent's position escapes me. It is even thinner than the soup Lincoln once described in 1858. Abraham Lincoln was at the time debating Stephen Douglas in a campaign for a seat in the United States Senate. Lincoln called Douglas's argument "as thin as the homeopathic soup that is made by boiling the shadow of a pigeon that had been starved to death."

Art—*Harmonious*

One very interesting test of art was once given by the French modern artist Marc Chagall. When a friend asked him how he knew a painting of his represented true art he replied, "When I judge art, I take my painting and put it next to a God-made object like a tree or flower. If it clashes, it is not art."

Art—*Performer*

Near the close of his life, Enrico Caruso wrote a letter to his wife in which were his last words: "I must give my soul to the public."

The performer tonight has also given her soul to the public. . . .

Aspiration—*Youth*

All of you can do as Ralph Waldo Emerson suggested: hitch your wagon to a star.

When Alexander Hamilton was a boy of twelve, living in the West Indies, he was a stock clerk in a store. Impatient and restless, he despised the mediocrity of his work and yearned in his dreams for the right outlet for his ambitions. In his diary he wrote these words: "I mean to prepare the way for futurity."

Assessment—*Contrast*

Alice Roosevelt Longworth's husband, Nicholas, was Speaker of the House, and almost as witty as she. Perhaps his most crushing rejoinder was directed at a presumptuous Congressman who passed his hand over Longworth's bald head and remarked, "Feels just like my wife's bottom." Longworth passed his own hand over his own head, and then said thoughtfully, "By golly, it does, doesn't it?"

Well, I can't say that the situation feels as smooth . . .

Assessment—*Empty*

Once Cardinal pitching ace Dizzy Dean was knocked unconscious by a hit through the mound. The inimitable Dean was taken to the hospital. The next day a headline read: "Dizzy Dean's Head X-rayed; Reveals Nothing."

Well, an accurate assessment of the head of this country has revealed nothing in the way of leadership . . .

Assessment—*Evaluation*

A real-estate agent once convinced Groucho Marx to take a look at a magnificent ocean-front estate that was up for sale. He drove Groucho up the long, lavishly landscaped driveway, took him on a tour of the mansion, the stables, the gardens, the kennels, all the while singing the praises of this palatial home by the sea. The comedian followed him about, nodding at the appropriate moments and apparently quite impressed by it all. Finally, the agent escorted Groucho out onto the veranda and, gesturing grandly toward the ocean, asked, "Now, what do you think?" "I don't care for it," replied Groucho. He motioned toward the view explaining, "Take away the ocean and what have you got?"

Well, in this case take away this lady's beauty and what have you got—just a brilliant mind . . .

⇌

When the argument is made that some parts of this program are good, I am reminded of what drama critic Alexander Woollcott had to say regarding a play others had reviewed in similar fashion. "To say of a bad play that some of it is pretty good is a little too much like saying of an unpleasant egg that at least part of it was fresh."

Assessment—*Liability*

Watching Pirate Dick Stuart bashing the ball for fantastic distances and then butchering the easiest kind of ground balls at first base, a sports writer for the Pittsburgh press said, "He's a Williams-type player: he bats like Ted and fields like Esther."

Well, our speaker today can both deliver a powerful speech and field questions—as he will demonstrate . . .

Associates—*Taint*

Frederick the Great of Prussia once visited a prison and interviewed the prisoners one by one. The monarch asked each of them what crime he had committed. They all declared themselves innocent of any misdeed whatsoever, except one man who owned up to the evil he had done, and admitted he was getting what he deserved. Frederick ordered his immediate release, saying, "This man obviously has no business here corrupting all these innocent people."

And in this group peopled by those of the purest motives we have one whose profession is admittedly base—he is a politician . . .

Attack—*Change*

George Earnshaw, the well-known Philadelphia right-hander of yesteryear, was pitching for Connie Mack's Athletics against the New York Yankees on a day when the famed Bronx Bombers of old were in a deadly slugging mood. Before a couple of innings had been played, Big George Earnshaw had had more than his share of trouble for one baseball day.

Among his chief tormentors was the late Lou Gehrig, who in his first two times at bat socked two home runs into the right-field stands. After the second homer, manager Connie Mack lost his patience and yanked the faltering pitcher out of the game. Disgusted with himself, Earnshaw started for the clubhouse but Connie Mack sharply called him back to the dugout and ordered him to sit down. "You sit right here next to me for the rest of this game.

I want you to watch how Mahaffey is going to pitch to that Gehrig fellow." Earnshaw plunked down on the bench, resigned to watch his successor hurl against the rampaging Yankees. Presently, up to bat again came Lou Gehrig, and this time he pickled the first pitch into the left-field stands for another home run. There was a long and awkward silence finally broken by Earnshaw, who turned to his manager and said, "I see perfectly what you mean, Mr. Mack. He sure made Gehrig change direction."

Well, the direction of the attacks on us has changed too. We used to be attacked from the left but now we find criticism from the right . . .

Attendance—*Communication*

I am happy to see such a nice crowd here today. I hope I convey my feelings better than Al Smith, who as Governor of New York was called upon during a visit to Ossining penitentiary, better known as Sing Sing, to speak to the convicts. The governor opened his speech by saying, "Fellow citizens—" A ripple of laughter sounded through the room. This rattled Al, so he started again. "Fellow convicts," he stammered. The pitch of the laughter rose higher. "Oh," he exclaimed in desperation, "you know what I mean. I'm glad to see so many of you here."

Seriously, I am glad to see . . .

Audience—*Minority*

Chicago White Sox impresario Bill Veeck is addicted to wearing a neat T-shirt and slacks, but on more formal occasions he adds a tweed jacket to the ensemble. Never will he don a necktie. Even when he was once invited to attend a formal dinner as guest of honor, Bill showed up in his usual dress. There was, of course, considerable murmuring from the many hundreds of tuxedoed gentlemen present. As Veeck got up to make his address, he noticed the frowns of disapproval in the audience. He grinned, then broke the icy silence by saying, "Well, folks, this is the first time I ever saw twelve hundred waiters for one lone customer!"

Well, in front of this audience of businessmen I feel like there must be twelve hundred Republicans listening to one lone Democrat . . .

Audience—*Occasion*

As I survey this crowd, I think of a situation that former Senator Joe Blackburn once faced. He was a guest at a barbecue in his home state of Kentucky. A friend found him disconsolate and withdrawn from the crowd.

"What's the matter, Joe, why are you crying?"

"It's the crowd" whimpered Joe.

"Now what's the matter with the crowd?"

"This crowd—it's breaking my heart."

"But they're all your old friends and supporters, Joe."

"I know that, but this crowd's too damned big for an anecdote, and not near big enough for an oration."

Audit—*Appearances*

Things are not always what they seem. That's why I say there has to be an investigation or check.

Maxfield Parrish, the famed illustrator who painted such huge frescoes as the one in the King Cole Bar at the St. Regis Hotel, in New York, had a difficult time getting down to work. Parrish specialized in painting voluptuous nudes, and one morning a lovely young model showed up at his studio to pose. "I don't feel like working right now," said Parrish. "Let's have a cup of coffee." No sooner had they sat down than the studio buzzer rang. Parrish answered it and quickly slapped his hand over the transmitter. "Young lady," he cried, "for God's sake, take your clothes off—my wife's coming up to check on me."

Authority—*Manners*

No matter what position we hold, we must never forget our manners. People respond to a real leader, not because of the command he has but because of his character. In 1865 when General Ulysses Grant moved his occupying army into Shiloh, he ordered a 7:00 P.M. curfew. One distinguished Southern lady, a Mrs. Johnson, was seen near the downtown headquarters around the curfew limit.

General Grant approached her and said, "Mrs. Johnson, it's a little dangerous out there. I am going to ask two of my officers to escort you home."

"I won't go," replied Mrs. Johnson determinedly.

Grant smiled, and went back to his headquarters and returned with an overcoat that covered his insignia and rank.

"May I walk with you, Mrs. Johnson?" asked Grant.

"Yes," replied Mrs. Johnson, "I'm always glad to have a gentleman as an escort."

She walked back with a man she saw as a gentleman not a general.

Award—*Gratitude*

As I accept this medal I think of an incident involving the late Sir Winston Churchill. A prominent woman in New York had the honor of entertaining the former prime minister in her East Side apartment. Since Churchill was arriving by train from Washington on Sunday to deliver a major luncheon address the next day, she decided on an informal Sunday night supper with a fare of cold fried chicken and champagne. When the hostess was offering her distinguished guest some chicken, Churchill asked for a "breast." The hostess laughed, saying, "Mr. Churchill, in this country we mostly use the terms 'white meat' or 'dark meat.'"

The next day a florist made a delivery to the hostess's apartment. She opened the box and found an orchid corsage. With the flower was Churchill's card with the inscription: "I'd be most obliged if you would pin this on your white meat."

Award—*Reciprocity*

In 1946 when Winston Churchill delivered his famous Iron Curtain Address in Fulton, Missouri, a ceremony was held earlier to dedicate a bust of the wartime prime minister. After the speech a buxom Southern belle barged up to Churchill and gushed, "Mr. Churchill, I traveled over a hundred miles this morning for the unveiling of your bust." Replied the gallant Churchill, "Madam, I assure you, in that regard I would gladly return the favor."

Although I won't be able to return the favor that way, I would like to extend . . .

Background—*Autobiography*

Since I am asked to say something about my background, I am reminded about what Abraham Lincoln said when he was asked to tell the story of his life. He replied, "It is contained in one line of Gray's *Elegy Written in a Country Church-Yard:* 'The short and simple annals of the poor.' "

Bankers—*Accountants*

There are two ways to look at bankers: the way they look at themselves—and the way others look at them. For example, President Abraham Lincoln was introduced to a delegation of financial bigwigs who had come to the capital to arrange credit to the nation in the Civil War. The Secretary of the Treasury made an introduction ending with the Biblical quotation "For where your treasure is, there will your heart be also." (Matthew 6:21)

Lincoln countered with this: "That may be true, Mr. Secretary, but Matthew also writes, 'Wheresoever the carcass is, there will be the eagles gathered together.' "

Beauty—*Perfection*

When I behold the young lady who is the object of our attentions this evening, I become almost speechless at the perfect loveliness of her face and figure. I am reminded of what Chief Justice Salmon P. Chase said on a similar occasion. While on a visit in the South after the Civil War, he was introduced to a very beautiful woman who prided herself upon her devotion to the "lost cause." Anxious that the Chief Justice should know her sentiments, she remarked as she gave him her hand, "Mr. Chase, you see before you a rebel who has not been reconstructed." "Madam," he replied with a deep bow, "reconstruction in your case would be blasphemous."

Beginning—*Challenge*

On February 11, 1861, President-elect Lincoln made his departure from his home in Springfield to begin the rail journey to Washington, where he was to be inaugurated a month later. Lincoln himself felt a premonition that this was the last time he would see Springfield. Standing on the rear platform of his railroad car, he bid the townspeople farewell, closing with these words: "Today I leave you. I go to assume a task more difficult than that which devolved upon General Washington. The great God which guided him must help me. Without that assistance I shall surely fail; with it, I cannot fail."

Let us with God's help begin this endeavor and meet a challenge that will demand the very best of us . . .

Beginning—*Crisis*

Gentlemen, we meet together today in a time of crisis, which brings to my mind a description first used by Pope Clement. A protégé of the apostle Paul, Clement, in the era of Christian martyrdom, wrote to the church at Corinth a letter urging it to surmount with faith the problems of persecution. In a call for unity that I heartily echo he urged the Corinthians to remember that "we all are in the same boat."

Beginning—*Era*

This occasion marks a new era. In that sense I feel like Goethe, who on the twentieth of September, 1792, when accompanying the Duke of Weimar to Paris on a military excursion, saw the finest army in Europe inexplicably repulsed at Valmy by some French militia. The German poet told his troubled friends, "At this place and on this day a new epoch in the history of the world begins, and we shall be able to say that we were present at its beginning."

Beginning—*Government*

What we are doing today is something new and different. It is a challenge in government not unlike that faced by the Puritan leader John Winthrop, who was Governor of the Massachusetts Bay colony. He called together the passengers on the flagship *Arbella* as they faced the task of building a new government in a new and perilous frontier. "We must always consider," Winthrop said, "that we shall be as a city upon a hill . . . the eyes of all people upon us."

Beginning—*Start*

It might be said that today represents only a start—a beginning. But my answer to that is what scientist Michael Faraday once said to Benjamin Disraeli. When Prime Minister Disraeli was shown a dynamo by Faraday, its inventor, Disraeli looked at this forerunner of all generators and said, "What good is this?" Replied Faraday: "What good is a baby, Mr. Disraeli?"

Brevity—*Message*

The newly appointed bishop to the court of Queen Victoria was anxious to make a favorable impression with his first sermon, and sought out Benjamin Disraeli for advice. "How long, Mr. Prime Minister, do you think my first sermon should last?" he inquired. "Well," answered the prime minister, "if you preach for forty minutes, Her Majesty will be satisfied; for thirty minutes, she will be delighted; if you preach for only fifteen minutes, Her Majesty will be enthusiastic!"

So, following the advice of Disraeli, I will keep my remarks very brief . . .

Brotherhood—*Humanity*

One day, Count Leo Tolstoy was stopped by a beggar who seemed weak, emaciated, and starving. The author searched his pockets for a coin but discovered that he was without a single penny. Taking the beggar's worn hands between his own, he said: "Do not be angry with me, my brother; I have nothing with me." The lined face of the beggar became illumined as he replied: "But you called me brother—that was a great gift."

By supporting this program we are reaching out as brothers . . .

Building—*Dedication*

When artist, sculptor, and architect Michelangelo was leaving Florence for Rome, he turned and took a last look back at the dome of the Cathedral and said, "Like it, I will not build, because better I cannot."

Similarly, I do not see how we could have built better . . .

Bureaucracy—*Government*

It is hard to know which is worse about bureaucracy—its inefficiency or its arrogance—the idea that government knows best. In 1961 there was a seminar at Tufts on government at which public officials and selected citizens gathered to listen to lectures by political science experts. One such academician was John Kenneth Galbraith, who arrived very late for his lecture, explaining that he had spent the week in Washington conducting "a series of ritualistic hearings on whether the support price for potatoes should be 14 cents a pound or 16 cents a pound before deciding to split the difference at 15 cents." After giving a five-minute summary of the lecture he was to have given, he opened the floor to questions. One questioner was Donald Whitehead, who asked whether government ever exercised arbitrary use of government power.

Galbraith turned on the questioner. "That sounds like a Republican. Are you Republican?" Whitehead admitted he was. Galbraith then said, "Give me an example of such an arbitrary use of government power." When Whitehead paused Galbraith pressed the question. "Come on, give me a specific example. Now you asked the question. Surely you must be able to give one example." With Whitehead still floundering, Galbraith said, "Really, don't you Republicans have any imagination. Just give me one case." Then Whitehead replied, "How about 'sitting in Washington conducting a series of ritualistic hearings on whether the support price for potatoes should be 14 cents a pound or 16 cents a pound before deciding to split the difference at 15 cents a pound'?"

Dr. Galbraith in anger strode off the platform without a reply.

⇌

When Franklin Roosevelt was first President, he found himself burdened by old files left by previous administrations. Repeatedly he called the State Department and asked if they could be removed to one of their storage sections. But the State Department gave him the run-around. They either promised to get back and never did. Or they said there was no room when he knew there had to be.

One day he took matters in his own hands. He had himself wheeled from the White House to the old Executive offices next door. With the Under-Secretary of State Sumner Welles accompanying him he made a surprise inspection at the close of the day's business.

At random, he picked an office halfway down the hall. F.D.R. entered without announcement to the consternation of State Department aides and clerks and picked the middle drawer in the first file cabinet he found. He opened a folder and read its title "Horses in China."

"I suppose this is an example of the top-priority files the State Department says can't be destroyed. Well, they can now—and the old files are coming over here," he said.

Bureaucracy—*Paranoia*

In his book about J. Edgar Hoover, *No Left Turns,* author Joseph L. Schott, an ex-FBI agent, writes about Hoover's idiosyncrasies. Once he was involved in an auto collision when his car made a left turn and he was sitting behind the driver. After that Hoover instructed the FBI to plan routes with no left turns. Once the author of the book had to plot a trip from Dallas to Austin with a special map showing no left turns. Hoover obviously went to great lengths to prove he was not a leftist.

There is a certain paranoia that affects career bureaucrats and it grows worse with years . . .

Bureaucrats—*Tenure*

The problem with bureaucracy is that agencies often outlive their purpose. The average bureaucrat is as tenacious as General Grant in holding to his niche.

General Grant was known for his stubbornness. Having once taken a place he never surrendered it. President Lincoln once commented on this to General Butler, saying, "When General Grant once gets possessed of a place he seems to hang on to it as if he had inherited it."

Business—*Ethics*

Dr. Samuel Johnson was once asked by a young nobleman what had become of the gallantry and military spirit of the old English nobility. Johnson replied, "Why, my lord, I'll tell you what has become of it; it has gone into the City to try to make a fortune."

Too many so-called gentlemen forget their manners as well as their ethics in dealing with competitors or consumers . . .

Business—*Failure*

Success in business is often the courage to recover from the last failure. In 1928 Paul Galvin, at the age of thirty-three, had already failed in business twice, being forced out of the storage-battery business by competition. Convinced he still had a marketable idea, he attended the auction of his own business and, with $750 he had managed to raise, bought back the battery eliminator portion of it. That was the beginning of Motorola. When he retired in the 1960s, he said, "Do not fear mistakes. You will know failure— continue to reach out."

Business—*Legality*

Some years ago John G. Johnson, the Philadelphia corporation lawyer, was retained by E. H. Harriman, one of those malefactors of great wealth whom Teddy Roosevelt was fond of berating. There came a time when Johnson's counsel was urgently required in connection with one of the colossal railroad mergers that Harriman specialized in sponsoring. A cable of prodigious length was dispatched to Johnson, narrating in minutest detail exactly what the project was. The point on which the railroad magnate and his associates needed guidance was whether the merger could be accomplished without subjecting its parties to federal prosecution under the Clayton Anti-Trust Act. Harriman requested Johnson to spare no words or expense in cabling his opinion, as the deal depended on it. An answer came within twenty-four hours. It read, in full: "Merger possible; conviction certain." By the way, for that opinion Johnson rendered Harriman a bill of $100,000—$25,000 a word.

Although that is not quite our situation—that what we would like to do is closely circumscribed by the law . . .

Business—*Marketing*

At the turn of the century an eager young man solicited the advice of the late Bernard Baruch. Although a young man himself, Baruch had already become a financial tycoon. "Tell me, is there any sure and certain way to make a million dollars?" asked the youth. "Yes, one," replied Baruch. "All you need do is buy a million bags of flour at a dollar a bag and then sell them for two dollars a bag." Baruch did not know that the young man, who grinned at the sally, took him seriously. And so it was that August Hecker went on to start the mighty Hecker's Flour Mills, at one time the largest company of its kind in the world.

The secret of marketing is still the key to profit . . .

Business—*Merchant*

When Napoleon was in exile a Britisher, visiting him, asked why the Emperor had slurred England by calling it "a nation of shopkeepers." Napoleon replied, "You were greatly offended with me for having called you a nation of shopkeepers. Had I meant by this that you were a nation of cowards, you would have reason to be displeased, even though it was ridiculous and contrary to historical facts, but no such thing was intended. I meant that you were a nation of merchants, and that all your riches and grand resources arose from commerce, which is true. What else constitutes the riches of England?"

Napoleon respected the British genius for business in the growing industrial age. Napoleon also knew that all great civilizations, including Periclean Athens, Renaissance Florence, and Victorian England, had their basis in trade.

Business—*Private Enterprise*

The House of Commons was regaled one day by a speech by a Laborite intellectual on the evils of free enterprise and the sins of the profit motive, and the corresponding glories of state socialism. At the end of the long tirade, Winston Churchill rose to respond. "The substance of the eminent Socialist gentleman's speech is that making a profit is a sin, but it is my belief that the real sin is taking a loss," he observed.

Capitalism, like the human body, is nothing to be ashamed of— yet too many businessmen today hide themselves in the bushes. It is time to stop being defensive about business and the profit incentive . . .

Business—*Salesmanship*

The great industrialist Charles Schwab was noted especially for inspiring an amazing degree of cooperation in people who worked with him, as well as in those with whom he had business dealings. When he was asked what he considered the prime ingredient in his character that had helped make him such a towering success, he answered, "I consider my ability to arouse enthusiasm among people the greatest asset I possess."

And salesmanship is still the greatest asset in marketing . . .

Business—*Stock Market*

The rector of the church which was attended by Jay Gould, the great Wall Street tycoon, was getting ready to retire and had managed to accumulate about thirty thousand dollars during his lifetime by scrimping and saving. He asked Gould for financial advice. "I'm going to tell you something with the understanding the information is for your ears only," said Gould. The preacher agreed. "Take your money and buy Missouri Pacific," said Gould.

The minister did and for some months the stock went up, and each day he was richer on paper. Then suddenly bad times came, and he was wiped out. Sadly he went to see Gould. "I took your advice and have lost all my savings," he reported.

"I am sorry," replied the great man. "You say the amount was thirty thousand dollars. To restore your faith, I am going to give you a check for forty thousand dollars." He wrote it out and handed it to him.

The minister looked at it reluctantly. "I must confess something," he began as he fumbled with the piece of paper. "I didn't keep my word to you, I told several members of the congregation." "Oh, I know that," replied Gould cheerfully. "They were the ones I was after."

Well, that story pretty much illustrates the machinations of some of the Wall Street types, and they haven't changed . . .

Cabinet—*Associates*

The Earl of Rochester, who was the favorite of Charles II, one day had the audacity to inscribe the following epigram on the door of the king's bedchamber: "Here lies our sovereign lord the King;/ Whose word no man relies on;/Who never said a foolish thing;/ And never did a wise one." When the king read the inscription he said, "True, my sayings are my own, but my doings are those of my ministers."

And, similarly, I am not going to hold myself accountable for the actions of my aides . . .

Calmness—*Leadership*

In 1848 when the Chartists began their demonstration Lord Salisbury, aide-de-camp to the Duke of Wellington, galloped in great anxiety to the duke at the Horse Guards and found him reading his morning paper. He lifted his head for a moment and said, "How far are they now from Westminster Bridge?" Lord Salisbury replied, "One mile and a half, sir." The great duke said, "Tell me when they are within a quarter of a mile," and became absorbed again in his paper. Lord Salisbury went back to observe. When the procession reached the appointed distance he galloped back to the Horse Guards and again found the Iron Duke quietly reading. "Well?" said the duke. Lord Salisbury reported that the procession was breaking up and that only small detached bodies of Chartists were crossing the bridge. "Exactly what I expected," said the duke, and returned to his paper.

Leadership is being prepared for any emergency by a thorough understanding of all possible contingencies . . .

Candidate—*Determination*

Like Abraham Lincoln I am not sure about everything, but I am sure of one thing—my political candidacy. When Lincoln ran for Congress in 1846 against Peter Cartwright, the Methodist hell-fire and damnation evangelist who spread the word that Lincoln was godless, Lincoln went to a revival meeting in Springfield where Cartwright said, "All who desire to give their hearts to God, and go to heaven, will stand." Many stood.

"All who do not wish to go to hell will stand." And everybody but Lincoln stood. "I observe that everybody but Mr. Lincoln indicated he did not want to go to hell. May I inquire of you, Mr. Lincoln, where are you going?" "Brother Cartwright asks me directly where I am going. I desire to reply with equal directness: I am going to Congress."

Candidate—*Posturing*

A delegation from Kansas, calling upon Theodore Roosevelt at Oyster Bay, was met by the President with coat and collar off. "I'm dee-lighted to see you," said the President, mopping his brow, "but I'm very busy putting in my hay now. Come down to the barn and we'll talk things over while I work." When they arrived at the barn there was no hay waiting to be thrown into the mow. "James!" shouted the President to his hired man in the loft. "Where's that hay?" "I'm sorry, sir," admitted James, poking his head out from the loft, "but I just ain't had the time to throw it back since you forked it up for yesterday's delegation."

And populist-posturing with blue jeans and earth shoes doesn't make a politician any less high-handed or arbitrary . . .

Capital—*Investment*

Walter van Tilburg Clark, author of *The Ox-Bow Incident,* visited a New England town to get background material for a new novel. One afternoon he was walking down the street with the town postmistress when he noticed a man whom everybody seemed to avoid as he approached in the opposite direction. "Who is this fellow?" asked Clark. "His name is Eustace Barron," she said icily, "and we don't talk about him in these parts." Clark's interest was whetted. Here was an intrigue that would be ideal material for a book. So Clark went to the editor of the local newspaper and asked, "Who is this man, a murderer, rapist, a pervert or what?" The editor tightened his lips and said, "Do you think I'd mind a little thing like that?" "Well, then, what is it?" "Okay, you asked for it," said the editor as he looked around to see if they were alone. "Eustace Barron," he whispered into Clark's ear, "dipped into his capital."

While I am not as tightfisted as our New England brethren, I do think we ought to think very carefully before committing ourselves to this venture . . .

Career—*Beginning*

When Methodist founder and hymnist Charles Wesley graduated from Oxford in 1730, he received this note from the rector of Epworth: "You are now launched fairly, Charles; hold up your head, and swim like a man, but always keep your eye fixed above the pole star."

Caring—*Remembrance*

Babe Ruth had hit 714 home runs during his career and this was his last full major-league game. It was the Braves versus the Reds in Cincinnati. The great Ruth, who had enjoyed the cheers and admiration of the throngs throughout the years, was no longer as agile as he had been. He fumbled the ball, he threw badly, and in one inning alone his misplays were responsible for most of the five runs scored by Cincinnati. As he walked off the field after the third out and headed toward the club house, a rising crescendo of yelling, hissing, and booing reached his ears. The one-time hero was angry and discouraged. Just then, a young boy jumped over the railing onto the playing field, and with tears streaming down his face, threw his arms about the knees of his hero. He wanted to share in the heartache of the man he admired. Ruth didn't hesitate for a second. He picked the boy up and hugged him. Suddenly the crowd went silent. The act of caring by a little boy shamed them into remembering the great slugger's heroic accomplishments of the past.

Cause—*Accumulation*

They say that an apple a day keeps the doctor away, but the immortal Babe Ruth, greatest home-run hitter of all time, never believed it. The "King of Swat" was king-sized in everything he did, even when it came to eating. He had a gargantuan appetite which he couldn't control even during working hours. Once, just before the start of a game, Babe sneaked in a couple of sandwiches, ate a dozen hot dogs, gulped down ten bottles of soda pop, and then topped off that hurried snack with an apple. After only a few innings of play, he caved in with a stomach ache that was heard around the baseball world. Headlines told an entire nation about Babe Ruth's belly ache. When the very sick and unhappy Babe was carted off to a hospital, he moaned, "I knew I shouldn't have et that apple."

Cause—*Complaint*

In the early 1960s the great Sir Winston Churchill, approaching ninety, was enjoying his declining years. He used to occasionally dine out with Lady Churchill at the Savoy Hotel. Once after Churchill's secretary made the eight P.M. reservation, a Savoy executive, Mrs. French, cancelled her plans for an opera night to observe the dinner at a discreet distance. The Churchills opened their meal with champagne and oysters. For a soup Sir Winston picked a pea puree washed down with a very fine sherry. Then they enjoyed poached turbot with a vintage bottle of French chablis. For the meat course Sir Winston and his wife split a rack of lamb and drank a bottle of claret. Following a salad, Churchill ate for his dessert a sherry trifle and with it drank a couple of glasses of rich Madeira wine. Then he ordered some cheese—good British Stilton along with some rare old port. Finally, he topped off the evening with a couple of glasses of cognac and a prewar Havana cigar. Since Mrs. French thought the evening was a culinary success, she was somewhat surprised the next morning when Churchill's private secretary called and said in his clipped voice, "Mrs. French, Sir Winston thinks there was something wrong with the oysters—he is feeling rather indisposed this morning."

Well, similarly, I don't see too much cause for complaint—whatever went wrong the record on our part shows . . .

Challenge—*Defeat*

The Chinese word for "crisis" is composed of two picture-characters—the one meaning "danger" and the other "opportunity." A good example of how opportunity can be found in danger is the story of Nathaniel Hawthorne. When he was dismissed from his government job in the custom house, he went home in despair. His wife after listening to his tale of woe, set pen and ink on the table, lit the fireplace, put her arms around his shoulders and said, "Now you will be able to write your novel."

Hawthorne did and literature was enriched with *The Scarlet Letter.* . . .

Challenge—*Pride*

In this challenging situation our very manhood is being tested. It is like the time Texas A & M was behind three touchdowns at half-time. Their coach, Dana Bible, addressed the team in the locker room just before the second half: "Well, girls, shall we go." The Aggies, with their manhood challenged, went out and won the game.

Change—*Adaptability*

The changing winds of politics demand constant adjustment. Lyndon Johnson was a superb politician all the time he was in the Senate. In 1953 he told a journalist friend that Vice President Nixon was "just chicken shit." The next week, Nixon returned from South America a mistreated national hero, and the first to hug him at the airport was Senator Johnson. The journalist reminded him of his earlier opinion of Nixon. "Son," Johnson replied, "in politics you've got to learn that overnight chicken shit can turn to chicken salad."

Change—*Assessment*

The assessment you have heard is correct as far as it goes. It is an accurate picture of general conditions but not as they apply to us. I might by way of example refer to some words of Abraham Lincoln. Stephen Douglas, his senatorial rival, was repeatedly making remarks about Lincoln's lowly station in life and saying that his first meeting with him had been across the counter of a general store. He finally ended his remarks by saying, "And Mr. Lincoln was a very good bartender, too." There was a roar of laughter at this, but it quieted down considerably when Lincoln said quietly: "What Mr. Douglas has said, gentlemen, is true enough; I did keep a grocery, and I did sell cotton, candles, and cigars, and sometimes whiskey; but I remember in those days that Mr. Douglas was one of my best customers. Many a time have I stood on one side of the counter and sold whiskey to Mr. Douglas on the other side, but the difference between us now is this: I have left my side of the counter, but Mr. Douglas still sticks to his as tenaciously as ever."

Change—*Mess*

Virginia Congressman John Randolph once said to a waiter at a Washington hotel as he handed him a cup and saucer, "Take that away—change it." "What do you want, Mr. Randolph?" asked the waiter respectfully. "If that stuff is tea, bring me coffee. If it's coffee, bring me tea. I want a change."

And whatever they call their program the clear fact is—it's not working. We need a change . . .

Change—*Rut*

Cecil Rhodes, the empire builder of South Africa, was once asked by a friend why he chose to come to Africa. "Well, they will tell you that I came on account of my health, or from a love of adventure—and to some extent that may be true; but the real fact is that I could no longer stand the cold mutton of an English supper."

Gentlemen, for the past years we have been in a rut too, not cold mutton maybe . . .

Character—*Introduction*

Protocol required Supreme Court Justice Hugo Black to attend the funeral of a man he had cordially detested for years. A colleague who was late for the services whispered in Justice Black's ear, "How far has the service gone?" Justice Black whispered back, "They just opened the defense."

The speaker today needs no defense. Even though protocol requires me to say nice things in an introduction, I and everybody else who has known him over the years say the same things behind his back . . .

Children—*Family*

There is no greater source of comfort than the family. Its love binds and sustains us. It is the hope for the future. Shortly before his death in January 1973, L.B.J., with his daughter Luci and grandson Lyn Nugent, was watching a TV documentary about Harry Truman. The five-year-old boy spoke up. "My grandpoppa has been very sick. How long do you think my grandpoppa will live?" Luci Johnson Nugent replied, "I hope grandpoppa lives to be a hundred. Don't you agree?" "No, ma'am," said the boy with the determination in his eyes like his grandfather, "I hope grandpoppa lives to infinity." His grandpoppa scooped him up and said, "I hope I live forever near you."

Choice—*Preference*

When Andrew Jackson was finishing his second term at the White House, various politicians were trying to sound him out on his choice for his successor. At first Jackson was noncommittal. Friends of John C. Calhoun became hopeful. Some of them called at the White House. When they pressed him, Jackson said he was "in favor of Van Buren." One of the inquisitors, not content, asked, "General, who then is your second choice?"

"By the Eternal," said Old Hickory, growing impatient, his eyes flashing with excitement, "by the Eternal, sir, I never had a second choice in my life."

And I can say my first choice to head this project . . .

Chore—*Enjoyment*

There are some chores that are onerous, others delicate—some, however, turn out to be delightful. Ambassador John Humes at the U.S. Embassy in Austria found himself in a difficult situation. He was the recipient of several boxes of Havana cigars. Since his country had no formal relations with Cuba, this gift could be embarrassing to an American diplomat. But he was resolute. He knew what had to be done. He gave his deputy chief of mission these instructions: "Burn them . . . one by one . . . slowly."

Church—*Clergy*

During the Brooklyn Dodgers-New York Yankees World Series of 1953, Cardinal Spellman put in an appearance in a front-row box along the third-base line. A high foul ball came in his direction with Dodger catcher Roy Campanella in hot but fruitless pursuit. The ball bounced on the railing and caromed onto the noted churchman's knee. Campanella took a split second out of the game to inquire respectfully if Cardinal Spellman had been hurt. "Don't worry about me, Roy," said His Eminence. "God had the wisdom to make a priest's knees the toughest part of his anatomy."

Church—*God*

One day the telephone rang in the office of the rector of President Franklin D. Roosevelt's church, St. John's Episcopal, which lies off Lafayette Square opposite the White House, and an eager voice said, "Tell me, do you expect the President to be in church this Sunday?" "That," explained the rector, "I cannot promise. But we expect God to be there, and we feel that will be incentive enough for a reasonably large attendance."

And with all due respect to the many distinguished dignitaries at this ecumenical conference, I think we know whose presence is responsible for the fine attendance . . .

Citizenship—*Businessman*

Each of us can help make our job a vocation, our town a community, our aspirations accomplishments. President Theodore Roosevelt had finished making a speech in Chicago when a member of the audience hesitatingly approached him, and said, "Mr. President, you have talked eloquently about the role of America in the twentieth century. But, Mr. President, what can I, as a small shopkeeper, do to help the country?" Replied T.R., "Do what you can with what you've got, where you are, but do it."

City—*Civic Pride*

The greatness of a city is measured not by its halls and parks but by its heart and pride. Some thousands of years ago a minister recommended to Lycurgus that he should enclose the city of Sparta within walls. The Greek statesman replied, "Any city is well fortified which has real men instead of brick."

I see in the audience today such men with civic pride and heart . . .

Civil Rights—*Justice*

Benjamin Franklin once said to Thomas Paine, "Where liberty is, there is my country." But Paine replied, "Where liberty is not, there is mine."

Today we honor a man like Thomas Paine, who has been involved in every cause to secure justice . . .

Claims—*Impossible*

During World War II when the draft thinned the ranks of professional baseball talent, a brash rookie tried out for the Chicago Cubs before Manager Charlie Grimm. "I'm 4F," said the kid, "and I can hit like Stan Musial, throw harder than Bob Feller, and play the field better than Joe DiMaggio. And if you need me I can coach at first base too." "You're crazy," was the reply by Charlie. "Sure," said the kid, "that's why I'm 4F."

And anyone offering the incredible promises and impossible claims of this congressional candidate has to be crazy too . . .

Closing—*Retirement*

Finally, I'd like to relate the advice once given to Senator Claude Swanson. The Virginia Senator could unwind a lengthy banquet speech. One night he labored far beyond his allotted time. As he was leaving the hall an elderly woman shook his hand. Swanson responded by asking her how she liked the speech. "I liked it fine," she said, "but it seems to me you missed several excellent opportunities." "Several excellent opportunities for what?" asked Swanson. "To quit," snapped the old lady.

Committee—*Dissent*

The laborious efforts of committee work to produce a single statement remind me of the frustrating hobby of Emperor Charles V. When the king of the Holy Roman Empire retired in weariness from the greatest throne in the world to the solitude of the monastery of Yuste in Spain he occupied his leisure for almost a year in trying to regulate and synchronize his collection of clocks. It proved very difficult. One day he turned to his assistant and said, "To think that I attempted to force the reason and conscience of thousands of men into one mold, and I cannot make even two clocks agree!"

Commitment—*Beginning*

This ceremony culminates many long months of work and sacrifice. We succeeded because we believed . . . because we had faith in the justice of our cause. . . . The commitment we have today recalls the White House ceremony to honor the signing of the Emancipation Proclamation.

President Lincoln, exhausted by endless handshaking and other traditional amenities, rested for a moment and remarked, "If my name goes down in history it will be for this one act. My whole soul is in it. If my hand trembles when I sign this proclamation, all who examine the document hereafter will say, 'He hesitated.' " But Lincoln's hand did not tremble, he did not hesitate.

Commitment—*Chore*

What we sorely need in this country is a greater degree of day-by-day devotion. Many a man who willingly risked his life in time of crisis has now become so indifferent that he won't even drive to the nearest polling place to register his vote.

King Paul of Greece once told university students he would wield a pick with them on road work. When they shouted that they wanted to die for Greece, he gently reproved them. "That's not enough," he declared. "You must be ready to work for Greece."

Commitment—*Service*

I accept this challenge with a sense of both apprehension and awareness—apprehension of the difficulties and awareness of the responsibilities involved. When I was considering whether to assume this assignment, I thought of some words of John Frémont. In the summer of 1856 Captain Frémont vacationed on the New Jersey shore. He was contemplating whether to try for the Republican nomination for President. It was a new party with little hope for electoral victory. Walking on the shore at night, he sighted in the distance a lighthouse with the form of a wrecked ship buried in the sand below it. He said to his wife, "Before us lies the wreck of dishonor or the light of mission. When mission calls, no one can turn down the call of his country."

Common Sense—*Experience*

Shortly after John Kennedy was elected President, his Vice President, Lyndon Johnson, met with his old mentor, Sam Rayburn, Speaker of the House. Johnson said, "Sam, you should see all the brains the President has rounded up in his cabinet and White House staff. Why, those that haven't graduated from Harvard are Ph.D.s—and some are both."

"Yes, Lyndon," said Speaker Sam, "but I wish just one of them had run once for sheriff in his home county."

There is no substitute for experience or common-sense judgment . . .

Communication—*Image*

In 1912 the U.S. Senate was debating the admission of New Mexico to statehood. Arguments against were that half the people did not speak English and that almost everybody was illiterate. Publisher William Randolph Hearst was pushing for statehood and he arranged for a carload of Congressmen to travel by rail to the southwestern territory. Hearst's man, Colonel Nicholas Sellers, had organized an effective demonstration of "representative" native opinion. He had on hand a six-foot-seven Navajo Indian named Hosteen. Gifted with a basso profundo voice, Hosteen would have been a persuasive figure if he had been able to speak English. He was seated on a platform before the assembled Congressmen and other guests—Sellers had himself wedged between Hosteen and a half-breed interpreter named José Platero. Platero had memorized an eloquent oration drafted by Sellers. The plan was that when Sellers unobtrusively nudged Hosteen, the Indian would speak. Upon another nudge, Hosteen would stop. It didn't matter whether the Indian recited the alphabet or counted to 100 in Navajo. All the audience would hear was his majestic bass voice. When introduced, the Indian rendered his booming "address." At the Colonel's nudge he stopped and the interpreter gave a moving oration about how the Indians revered these white men from Washington whence all blessings came. Then Sellers nudged the Indian and he began his peroration again. At the end the delegation, many weeping, stood and applauded. They went back to Washington and voted for statehood.

Communication—*Instructions*

General Ulysses Grant was not known as a vain man, but one thing he prided himself on was his mastery of the English language. And his literary prowess was proved when his memoirs were published and became a best seller. He once told his son, General Frederick Dent Grant, that despite his many victories, his greatest achievement was that in all the orders he wrote in the Civil War, only one was misunderstood. "Son," he said, "the cardinal duty of a commanding officer in war is to be so precise in his use of words that nobody can misconstrue his orders."

The misunderstood order was to General Lew Wallace at the Battle of Shiloh to proceed by the River Road. At the time he wrote the order Grant didn't know that there were two roads locally called the River Road. Wallace took the wrong one. Wallace was court-martialed for it and General Grant appeared in his defense. Wallace was acquitted.

Communication—*Listening*

Most problems of communication result from not really listening. For instance, Mark Twain met Winston Churchill in 1900, when the latter was just coming into prominence as a young statesman. The occasion was a dinner in London. Churchill and Twain went out for a brief time to have a smoke. When the two men returned, Churchill was asked whether he had enjoyed himself, and the young man replied, "Yes," most enthusiastically. Then Twain was asked the same question. Twain hesitated and said, "Well, I have had a good smoke."

Communication—*Mistake*

Before we jump to conclusions, perhaps we should look at what was really said. It recalls the time in the FBI when an assistant's memorandum so filled the page that Mr. Hoover barely had room for a comment on the margin. He wrote, "Watch the borders," and his puzzled but obedient aides dispatched agents to patrol the Canadian and Mexican borders for a week.

Communication—*Silence*

Justice John Marshall Harlan used to play golf at the Chevy Chase Club outside Washington with his friend, the Episcopal Bishop of Washington. Once the Bishop missed the ball several times, but made no comment. However, he looked a picture of disgust. "Bishop," said Harlan, "that was the most profane silence I ever witnessed."

Communication—*Simplicity*

The secret of communication lies in simple, direct language. This is a fact that lawyers and bureaucrats do their best to ignore. President Roosevelt in 1942 learned that Civil Defense authorities during the wartime blackout had posters printed for distribution that read: "Illumination must be extinguished when premises are vacated." F.D.R. thundered, "Damn, why can't they say 'Put out the lights when you leave.' "

Communication—*Technology*

At a ceremony commemorating the laying of the Atlantic cable by Cyrus Field in 1866, Secretary of State William Evarts said, "Columbus said, 'There is one world, there shall be two.' Cyrus W. Field said, 'There are two worlds—there shall be one.' "

Since that time that one world has become smaller and smaller . . .

Comparison—*Introduction*

While I am not unappreciative of the comparisions made in the introduction, I can't help but wish that I had the gentleman's talents and looked like someone else. In that sense I feel like Paul Henri Spaak, the bald, portly, horn-rimmed bespectacled Belgian prime minister, who was former president of the U.N. General Assembly and former head of NATO. Spaak, who was often reminded of his resemblance to Winston Churchill, once commented on the comparison this way: "Oui," said the French-speaking Spaak, "zey say I look like Veenston Churcheel and speak like Charles Boyer. But I much prefer to speak like Veenston Churcheel and look like Charles Boyer."

Compassion—*Kindness*

When his nephew Billy, William James's son, came for a visit in 1902, Henry James told him: "Three things in human life are important. The first is to be kind. The second is to be kind. And the third is to be kind."

The work of the next speaker bespeaks such kindness . . .

Compassion—*Sensitivity*

When Baron Friedrich von Hügel, the great philosopher, mystic, and saint, was dying, his niece bent over him to hear what his moving lips were trying to say. She put her ear close against his mouth and heard this, the last words that great saint ever uttered: "Caring is everything, nothing matters but caring."

And caring exactly describes the program we offer . . .

Competition—*Battle*

When tough Early Wynn was a youthful fire-baller with the Washington Senators his manager, Bucky Harris, decided to start him against the Yankees. The veteran Yankee outfielder Ben Chapman looked into the visitors' dugout on his way to the outfield. "Hey, Bucky," he shouted, "I hear you're pitching that kid, Wynn. I figure to get five hits." "If you get five hits," snarled Wynn, "you'll get the last four lying on your back."

And I assure you we are going to give no quarter, or give away no advantage in our efforts . . .

Competition—*Planning*

It's like the time in the 1930s when the St. Louis Cardinals had the brothers Dizzy and Daffy Dean as pitchers. Once they played a double-header. Dizzy pitched the first game and hurled a brilliant two-hitter. Then Daffy pitched the second game and turned in a no-hitter. The sportswriters went to Dizzy and asked how he felt about having his brother outdo him. "Hell," said Dizzy, "if I'da knowed he was gonna pitch a no-hitter, I woulda throwed one, too!"

Well, if we'd a knowed our friends was gonna throw a party like this, we'd a throwed one too . . .

Competitor—*Cost*

Benjamin Franklin had the tenacity of purpose to succeed in business. When he started in the printing business in Philadelphia, he carried his materials through the streets on a wheelbarrow. He hired one room for his office, workroom, and sleeping room. He found a formidable rival in the city and invited him to his room. Pointing to a loaf of bread, part of which he had just eaten for his dinner, he said, "Unless you can live cheaper than I can, you cannot starve me out."

Ben knew the way to beat competition is to cut down costs . . .

Completion—*Perfection*

A visitor was admiring a painting in the studio of Renoir, who was noted for the voluptuousness of his nudes. "How do you achieve such perfect flesh tints?" he asked the artist. "I don't know myself," said Renoir. "I keep adding a stroke here and a stroke there." "But how do you know when it is exactly right?" "When I feel like pinching," confided Renoir.

Completion—*Thoroughness*

Whatever our speaker undertakes he does it completely— whether it's running a campaign or having fun. In that sense he is not unlike an old-time baseball star by the name of Paul Waner. For almost two decades he was one of the greatest outfielders in the game, and he was one of the most remarkable batters of all time. During his fabulous big-league career with the Pittsburgh Pirates, Paul Waner made more than three thousand hits. However, although he was one of the greatest ball players that ever lived, off the field he was hardly a model for the Boy Scouts. Paul Waner's escapades in search of fun used to drive Frankie Frisch, manager of the Pirates, wild.

One afternoon, manager Frisch found a bottle of whiskey in the clubhouse and he confronted Paul Waner with it, as he roared in anger, "Waner, is this your bottle?" Paul Waner nonchalantly inquired, "Is there anything in it?" "Is there anything in it? You bet there is!" screamed Frankie Frisch. "This whiskey bottle is full!" Paul Waner simply shrugged his shoulders and replied. "Then it's not mine! If it was—the bottle would be empty."

Complexity—*Incomprehensible*

Some years ago Professor Albert Einstein and Dr. Chaim Weizmann sailed together to America on a Zionist mission. When they arrived in New York City Dr. Weizmann was asked how he and the famous savant had spent their time on the boat. "Throughout the voyage," Dr. Weizmann replied, "the learned professor kept on talking to me about his theory of relativity." "And what is your opinion about it?" "It seems to me," concluded Dr. Weizmann, "that Professor Einstein understands it very well."

And, similarly, while I understand the greatness of our speaker, I can't say I really understand the nature of his work . . .

Complexity—*Insoluble*

The British statesman Lord Palmerston once said of the Schleswig-Holstein question which led to the war between Prussia and Austria: "Only three men ever understood it. The first was Prince Albert, who is dead, the second was a Danish minister who had gone mad, and the third was myself and now I've forgotten."

Similarly, the origins of this dispute are quite involved. Well,

I assure you, I wish I had forgotten because I almost went mad . . .

Compromise—*Endorsement*

At the end of the Constitutional Convention in 1787 the aging Benjamin Franklin rose and made this statement: "I agree to this constitution with all its faults—can a perfect constitution be expected? I consent to this constitution because I expect no better because I am not sure it is not the best."

Similarly, I will support this program . . .

Compromise—*Limit*

When General Benjamin Lincoln in the early nineteenth century went to make peace with the Creek Indians, one of the chiefs asked him to sit down on a log. He was then asked to move, and in a few minutes to move still further. The request was repeated till the general got to the end of the log. The Indian said, "Move further," to which the general replied, "I can move no further." "Just so it is with us," said the chief, "you moved us back to the waters, and then ask us to move further."

Likewise we have gone far enough . . .

Compromise—*Qualifications*

Groucho Marx applied for membership in a California athletic club since he wished his children to enjoy the privileges of its swimming pool. He was turned down because the club did not admit Jews. Upon receiving the rejection slip Groucho wrote to the president: "Sir, it is not my wish to have you change the rules of your organization. However, since my children are only half Jewish, I request that you grant them a special permit to enable them to go into the pool up to their navels."

And, similarly, since I can only qualify halfway I think I ought to be allowed in this group to . . .

Conceit—*Ego*

When that great film classic *Citizen Kane* was being shot in the late 1930s, Orson Welles was all over the lot, doing the jobs of producer and director as well as actor in the title role. Once when the looming presence of Welles made itself felt on the set, writer Herman J. Mankiewicz made this side comment: "There, but for the grace of God goes God."

⊽

The pious Donald Fleming, finance minister of Canada under the Diefenbaker government, got under some liberal skins. Once, after Fleming told the Canadian House of Commons of his arduous and diligent dedication to the people of Canada, the remarks prompted James Sinclair, the Liberal financial critic, to whisper sotto voce, "If conceit is the small man's sword, Don is the best-armed man in Canada."

And by that standard our friend who wields the vertical pronoun like a battering ram is a walking armory . . .

Concern—*Needs*

Once at one A.M. the telephone of Harry Emerson Fosdick, the celebrated preacher, rang. He answered, expecting to hear of an emergency of some sort for which his help was being sought. "Is this Dr. Fosdick?" a rather inebriated-sounding voice asked. Dismayed, the minister said, "Yes, this is Dr. Fosdick speaking." "Dr. Harry Emerson Fosdick?" "Yes, yes," was the impatient answer. "What is it you want?" "Dr. Fosdick, I want to know the difference between Fundamentalism and Modernism." Exasperated, Dr. Fosdick said, "God heavens, man, that's not something I can explain to you over the telephone, and obviously you're in no condition to hear. Come around to my study tomorrow and I'll be glad to answer your questions." "But, Dr. Fosdick," insisted the voice, "I can't wait until tomorrow. I must know now." Angrily Dr. Fosdick said, "Why can't you wait until tomorrow? Why do you have to know now?" "Because," said the voice patiently, "tomorrow I won't give a damn."

And, gentlemen, we have to be there when we are needed. It doesn't matter how much we could offer unless we can provide it at their convenience . . .

Conciliation—*Accommodation*

In the long run I think we would be better served by a conciliatory approach. I recall once when Abraham Lincoln was criticized for referring to the Confederates in kind terms. The woman critic asked the President how he could speak generously of his enemies when he should rather destroy them.

"Why, Madam," replied Lincoln "do I not destroy them when I make them my friends?"

Conditional—*Vice*

Gene Hermanski and Chuck Connors, now a TV star, came up to the Dodgers together. They met in the anteroom of the Dodger front office, and Hermanski went in to see Branch Rickey first. After an hour or so, he came out and Connors asked him how it went. "Everything was going along all right," said Gene, "until he asked me if I drank. I said a little now and then, and he hit the ceiling." Forewarned, Connors went in to see the Holy Man, who fired the same questions at him. "Do you smoke?" "No, Mr. Rickey." "Do you go out with women?" "No, Mr. Rickey." "Do you drink?" Connors brought his fist down on the desk and shouted, "If I have to drink to stay in your organization I'm leaving!"

Conference—*Negotiation*

The late Ramsay MacDonald, former prime minister of Britain, was discussing the possibility of lasting peace with another government official. The latter was unimpressed with the prime minister's viewpoint. "The desire for peace," he said cynically, "does not necessarily insure peace." "Quite true," admitted MacDonald. "Neither does the desire for food satisfy hunger.

But at least it gets you started toward a restaurant."

At least by today's conference we take a step . . .

Conference—*Schedule*

When the late Herman Hickman was coaching football at Yale, he began the daily practice sessions at four P.M. The players, with heavy scholastic schedules, frequently came late. More often than not, the entire squad would not be assembled until four-thirty. Hickman, a stickler for punctuality, worried about this loss of precious time. Then he hit on a way to beat the problem. When all the players had arrived, no matter what the time, he would turn the clock back to four and practice would begin.

Unfortunately, the conference chairman won't allow me to do this, so I would ask . . .

Conference—*Seminar*

George Bernard Shaw was once invited to speak at a seminar where the presentations had been far too many and far too long for the patience of the audience. They waited expectantly for Shaw, who was last to speak. When the roar of applause had subsided, he said, "Ladies and gentlemen, the subject is not exhausted, but we are," and sat down.

Well, although there is much more we could say, time is running late . . .

Confidence—*Faith*

When Rear Admiral Samuel Francis Du Pont explained to his superior officer, Admiral David Farragut, the reason why he had failed to take his ships into Charleston Harbor in 1863, Farragut heard him through to the end and then said, "Admiral, there is one explanation which you have not given." "What is that?" asked DuPont. "It's this. You did not believe that you could do it."

If we have faith in the rightness of our cause, we will not fail . . .

Congress—*Government*

In 1909 when a Minneapolis baseball team played Kansas City at Kansas City the umpire was Clarence Owens. Watching was an honored guest—the Vice President of the United States, James S. Sherman. At one point when Kansas City was about to get a big batting rally going, Umpire Owens called a Kansas City player out at first on a close play. Immediately a messenger came onto the field and informed Owens that "Mr. Sherman would like to speak to you in his box." Umpire Owens walked over to the box where Vice President Sherman was seated. "Mr. Owens," said Sherman, "I believe your decision on that play was incorrect. The man was safe. Your umpiring has been good up to this point, but I am convinced that you made a mistake in this particular instance."

Umpire Owens reflected a moment. "Well, Mr. Sherman," he said, "it's quite possible that I did make a mistake. You know, baseball is a good deal different kind of business than running the government. Folks in the baseball business do sometimes make errors. But back there in Washington, where they make the laws and run the government, they never make any mistakes."

Vice-President Sherman seemed perplexed at first over this and then said, "No, I think we in Washington make a lot more mistakes than any umpire."

Congress—*Legislation*

Thomas Jefferson, who did not attend the Constitutional Convention, was not happy with the proposed bi-cameral system for the legislative branch of our government. One day Jefferson visited George Washington at Mount Vernon. In the course of their conversation Jefferson argued for the French uni-cameral system. After much discussion around the tea table, Washington turned sharply to Jefferson and said, "You, sir, have just demonstrated the superior excellence of the bi-cameral system by your own hand."

"Oh, how is that?" asked Jefferson.

"You have poured your tea from your cup out into the saucer to cool. We want the bi-cameral system to cool things. A measure originates in one house, and in heat is passed. The other house will serve as a wonderful cooler, and by the time it is debated and modified by various amendments there, it is much more likely to become an equitable law. No, we can't get along without the saucer in our system."

Well, in that respect I hope the Senate can "cool off" or least modify the recent bill . . .

Conscience—*Ethics*

I am not sure ethics can be translated into a code of law—it is a personal thing. You can be legal and still immoral.

Abraham Lincoln came under criticism for many things, including his religious beliefs. When a friend inquired about the matter of religion, the President remarked, "When I do good, I feel good; when I do bad, I feel bad; and that's my religion."

Conscience—*Excellence*

Pianist Ignace Paderewski was once asked why he religiously practiced six hours every day. "If I miss one day's practice," said he, "I notice it. If I miss two days, the critics notice it. If I miss three days, the audience notices it."

When we fall short of our own standards, we know it in our own hearts even if our friends, family, and associates don't notice it . . .

Conscience—*Expediency*

As an argument against expediency Abraham Lincoln told one of his best stories. Lincoln began his political career as a Whig, and he first crossed swords with George Forquer, who had left the Whigs to accept a Democratic appointment as register of the land office, a post that paid $3,000 a year and enabled him to build a fancy house with a lightning rod, still a novelty in Illinois. When Forquer attacked Lincoln after Lincoln had spoken in Springfield, Lincoln replied, "I desire to live, and I desire place and distinction; but I would rather die now than, like the gentleman, live to see the day that I would change my politics for an office worth $3,000 a year and then feel compelled to erect a lightning rod to protect a guilty conscience from an offended God."

And the course I suggest may not be the expedient or easy course, but, at least, we would have the comfort of sleeping restfully with an untroubled conscience . . .

Conscience—*Professional*

When the Athenian sculptor Phidias was carving the statue of Athena to be placed in the Acropolis and was working on the back of the head, he was careful to bring out, with his chisel, every strand of hair, as far as possible. Someone watching remarked: "That figure is to stand a hundred feet high, with its back to the marble wall. Who will ever know what details you are putting behind there?" Phidias replied, "I will know." And he continued with his detailed chiseling.

And we know in our own hearts when we don't do a truly professional job . . .

Controversy—*Publicity*

Bernard Shaw's name first became familiar to the general public as a result of scurrilous attacks, disguised as interviews, made upon him by a section of the London evening press. Apparently the interviewer would force his way into Shaw's apartment for no other purpose than to attack his views. Many people maintained that Shaw must be an imaginary person. Why did he stand for it? Why didn't he kick the interviewer downstairs? Failing that, why didn't he call the police? It seemed difficult to believe in the existence of a being so able to withstand such abuse as this poor persecuted Shaw. Everyone talked about him. Actually, the interviews were written by Shaw himself.

Now, similarly, in the case of our friend, much of the controversy is self-generated. He has not been shy about publicity . . .

Controversy—*Commitment*

Count Mirabeau, the eighteenth-century French statesman, received many challenges to duels. He always told the second who delivered the challenge: "Tell your principal, his favor is received and that his name is on my list. But I warn you that the list is long and that I grant no preferences."

Well, I am not afraid if I make any enemies by my outspokenness on this issue . . .

Conviction—*Determination*

Near the close of his illustrious career Winston Churchill went back to his old school, Harrow. He entered his old classroom where scores of young Harrovian students greeted the seventy-eight-year-old prime minister. With the encouragement of their cheers, Churchill mounted one of the pupil chairs and delivered a short valedictory address. "Never give in," he exhorted his young listeners. "Never, never, never, never, never give in except to convictions of honor and good sense."

With similar resolution let us pledge never to end our fight to . . .

Corruption—*Retraction*

Once Thaddeus Stevens, the Radical Republican, had gone to advise President Lincoln that Simon Cameron should not be appointed Secretary of War. "You don't mean to say you think Cameron would steal?" Lincoln asked. "No," was Stevens's reply, "the only thing he wouldn't steal is a red-hot stove." Lincoln repeated this comment to Cameron as a warning. Cameron, angered, asked for a retraction. Stevens, prodded by Lincoln, called at the White House and made his retraction this way: "I believe I told you Cameron would not steal a red-hot stove. I now take that back. He would."

Well, I may rephrase my language a little like Thaddeus Stevens, but like him I still stand by the essential thrust of what I said . . .

Courage—*Award*

After the defeat of Napoleon, the Prussian General, Blücher, refused the Order of the Holy Ghost, which the French King Louis

XVIII wished to confer. His friend the Duke of Wellington for the reasons of diplomacy tried in vain to persuade him to accept. "If I do," said the vengeful Prussian, "I will hang the order on my ass." "And if you do," observed the Iron Duke, "you will show how much you value it, by hanging it on the backside where the enemy will never hit it."

And, similarly, the man we honor today never ran from a fight . . .

Courage—*Defeat*

In 1969 the writer André Malraux visited the dying Charles de Gaulle at his home at Colombey-les-deux-Églises. Malraux told the general, "Dying never has interested me or you. We belong to those people who are indifferent to being killed."

Similarly, I can accept defeat because I have fought for principles . . .

Courage—*Resolution*

In 1775 the first American colonists to stand up against the British were the farmers from Concord and Lexington, Massachusetts. A militia captain, Isaac Davis of Acton, was asked whether he was ready to resist the British army. Said Captain Davis, "I haven't a man that's afraid to go."

And, similarly, we have an organization—united and ready to go . . .

Courage—*Risk*

When James B. Conant was president of Harvard University, he kept among other objects on his desk a little model of a turtle, under which was the inscription "Consider the turtle. He makes progress only when he sticks his neck out."

Accordingly, I plan to stick my neck out by making this promise . . .

Courage—*Stamina*

Real courage is not impulsive bravado. Far nobler is unyielding stamina. When James J. Corbett, former world heavyweight champion, was asked what was the most important thing a man must do to become a champion, he replied, "Fight one more round."

Creativity—*Compulsion*

It is not easy to turn on the creative juices. Carl Sandburg had the best answer about that. A newspaper reporter called him to confirm a rumor that he had been commissioned by a magazine to write another poem about Chicago. Sandburg answered, "Ordering a man to write a poem is like commanding a pregnant woman to give birth to a redheaded child. You can't do it—it's an act of God."

Creativity—*Insight*

Sir Joshua Reynolds, the great British portrait artist and master of reproducing subtle tones of flesh and clothes, was once asked, "What do you mix your colors with?" His reply was quick: "With brains."

Similarly, observation without insight is not enough . . .

Crime—*Mistake*

I would say as Joseph Fouché, the Duke of Otrante, when he heard the report that the Duke of Enghien had been executed by orders of the Directory. Fouché, himself a minister of police, said, "It is more than a crime—it is a blunder."

Criticism—*Blame*

As the late Chicago Mayor Dick Daley said when he was attacked for running a political machine, "They have vilified me—they have crucified me. Yes, they have even criticized me."

Well, I have come in for my share of criticism, but I regard that as a small price to pay for the privilege of standing up and fighting for what I think is right . . .

Criticism—*Complexity*

Once when Leo Durocher was manager of the Dodgers, he was booed for pulling out the pitcher in the eighth inning of a close ball game. After the game, a reporter asked him how he reacted to the crowd's disapproval. Leo said, "Baseball, you know, is like church. Many attend, but few understand."

Similarly, while everybody was aware of the decision I took the other week, few understood the complexity of the background at that time . . .

Criticism—*Inaccuracy*

On one occasion the historian and politician Thomas Macaulay had an unpleasant experience at Edinburgh. He was re-contesting a seat in that constituency, and was standing side by side with his opponent on a balcony one evening, when he was suddenly struck by a dead cat. The member of the audience who threw the animal at once apologized and said that he had intended it for his opponent. "Well," said Macaulay, "I wish you had meant it for me and struck him."

Well, the critics have been just as inaccurate in singling me out for something I didn't do . . .

Criticism—*Invective*

To answer such abusive charges it is only necessary to remember the religious leader Buddha. Once when Buddha was attacked and abused by a critic, he asked the attacker a hypothetical question: "If a man refuses the offer of a present, to whom does the present belong?" The man said, "The original donor." Thus Buddha turned aside criticism.

Criticism—*Irrationality*

William Howard Taft once met with some unfriendly elements at an outdoor rally he was addressing in Ohio. During the speech a few of them started to hurl things at him. Finally a big head of cabbage lobbed up toward him and fell at his feet. Taft leaned down, picked it up and said, "I see that one of my hecklers has lost his head."

And at least figuratively I think some of our Democratic friends have lost their heads in saying . . .

Criticism—*Self-Examination*

Woodrow Wilson, former President of the United States, was the son of a minister. His father, who was tall and thin, would often take his son with him, in his horse and buggy, as he made his pastoral calls. One day a parishioner asked, "Pastor, how is it that you're so thin while your horse is so fat?" Before the father could reply, Woodrow said, "Probably because my father feeds the horse and the congregation feeds my father!"

The point is that we shouldn't criticize unless we examine our own hearts first . . .

Criticism—*Response*

I have a copy of the gentleman's statement and I have a mind to do with it what Tallulah Bankhead once did. In answer to a highly uncomplimentary review of a performance, the actress wrote this note to the critic: "I am sitting in the smallest room of the house. Your review is before me. Soon it will be behind me."

Criticism—*Stupidity*

As I listen to the verbal rampage of this critic, I can console myself with the words of Senator George Vest. Years ago, in the dying moments of a losing debate, a certain Senator turned on Vest and denounced him viciously. When the tirade had ended, Vest rose slowly and silenced his opposition with this classic rejoinder: "Mr. President, after listening to the remarks of my learned colleague, I feel somewhat like the little corporal in the Philistinian army who, after Samson had passed through, picked himself off the ground and, holding his battered head, cried out, 'Now I know what it feels like to be smitten by the jawbone of an ass.'"

My reaction to the criticism of that particular party is much the same as that of Winston Churchill, when one day in the House of Commons, a Socialist poured out abusive words against the prime minister. Churchill remained impassive—almost bored. When the harangue was over, Churchill rose and said, "If I valued the opinion of the honorable gentleman, I might get angry."

Criticism—*Timing*

Following his support of the Compromise of 1850 in his famous March 7 speech, Daniel Webster was castigated as few men in history. Asked if he was going to reply to the abuse, Webster said he felt like the deacon who in similar circumstances told a friend, "I make it a rule never to shovel out the path until the snow is done falling."

Similarly, I am not going to comment until . . .

Crusader—*Advocate*

A grandson of Thomas Jefferson once asked a contemporary of his grandfather how he ranked as an orator. "Well," replied the old Virginian, who had served under the third President, "it is hard to say because your grandfather always took the right side."

And, similarly, our speaker has been in the forefront of a host of right causes . . .

Culture—*Choice*

My thoughts about either possibility are unenthusiastic—and I think of the time Robert Benchley sat down at a table in a bistro one night before the unlamented death of Prohibition and found himself in the midst of a discussion about the comparative unendurability of writers and artists. Someone asked, "If two ships were sailing from New York tonight, one filled with writers and the other with artists, which would you get on?" "Do I have to get on either one of them?" Benchley asked.

Culture—*Creativity*

The enduring monuments of society are far more often the work of the artist and intellectual than of the businessman and general.

For example, General James Wolfe, invading by rowboat down the St. Lawrence River in 1759, recited from memory to the crew the words of Gray's *Elegy Written in a Country Church-Yard.* One stanza was especially fitting:

> The boast of heraldry, the pomp of pow'r,
> And all that beauty, all that wealth e'er gave,
> Awaits alike th' inevitable hour.
> The paths of glory lead but to the grave.

Then General Wolfe said, unaware that he would die in the next day's victorious conquest of the French on the Plains of Abraham, "I'd rather be the poet who wrote these words than the general who took Quebec."

Danger—*Alert*

Just after the hapless expansion team the Seattle Pilots had been crushed by the Minnesota Twins, a few Pilots players were driving back to their hotel when their car was held up by a long funeral procession. As the long line of limousines continued to roll past, one of the players turned to pitcher Jim Bouton and said, "Who do you suppose that is—some big shot?" "Perhaps," answered Bouton, "but more likely it's some first baseman who thought Harmon Killebrew was going to lay down a bunt."

Well, we are going to be facing some big guns in this next operation . . .

Decisiveness—*Leadership*

Harry S. Truman used to recount a story about Adlai Stevenson. He was in the wings of a convention hall awaiting his turn to speak. He turned to his aide and said, "Do I have time to go to the bathroom?" and then, "Do I really have to go to the bathroom?"

Well, a real leader has to know where he wants to go and how he wants to go about it . . .

Decline—*Corruption*

When Raphael was engaged in painting his famous frescoes in the Vatican he was visited by two cardinals who began to criticize his work and find fault without understanding it. "The Apostle Paul has too red a face," said one. "He blushes to see into whose hands the Church has fallen," answered the angry artist.

And I think the founders of that institution would be ashamed to see the state . . .

Decline—*Retirement*

A young lady who had recently acquired a large fortune invited Ignace Paderewski to give a private concert at her home. Her knowledge of music was by no means as large as her newly found wealth. Commenting on one of his selections, she exclaimed, "What a beautiful piece. Who composed it?" "Beethoven, madam," was the reply. "Ah, yes," she said knowingly, "and is he composing now?" "No," replied Paderewski gravely, "he is decomposing."

Well, fortunately although I am no longer active, I have not quite yet begun to decompose . . .

Dedication—*Work*

One evening when Thomas Edison came home from work, his wife said to him, "You've worked long enough without a rest. You must go on a vacation." "But where on earth would I go?" asked Edison. "Just decide where you would rather be than anywhere else on earth," suggested the wife. Edison hesitated. "Very well," he said finally, "I'll go tomorrow." The next morning he was back at work in his laboratory.

Well, we don't all have to be workaholics like Thomas Edison, but we should enjoy our work and feel purpose in what we do . . .

Defeat—*Attitude*

After a British setback in the Boer War, Prime Minister Arthur Balfour was called to Buckingham Palace. Balfour tried to explain the South African situation to Queen Victoria. Victoria coldly replied, "We are not interested in the possibility of defeat."

Similarly, we are going to act as if we are going to win. If we do that, we shall prevail . . .

Defeat—*Battle*

Rogers Hornsby is as well known for his blunt manner of speech as he ever was for the mean and authoritative bat he carried to the plate. On one occasion, Hornsby came to bat against the Brooklyn Dodger ace Dazzy Vance, and the Dazzler struck out the great hitter three times in succession and held him to a meek little pop-up his fourth time up. As the Rajah made his disconsolate way back to the bench, a fan got up in the stands. "Hey, Hornsby!" yelled the fan. "Ya bum ya, I paid good dough to see ya hit!" "What're you squawking about?" demanded Hornsby. "You paid to see that fellow Vance pitch too, didn't you? You're sure getting your money's worth!"

Well, in this last battle I may have been defeated, but we gave everybody their money's worth . . .

Defeat—*Ending*

In the past many years I have watched this movement begin, rise, decline, and end. I feel the way Henry Grattan did. This Irish statesman, observing in 1801 the end of the parliament in Dublin and with it the cause of Irish independence, said, "I sat by its cradle, I now follow its hearse."

And yet, as in Ireland, I am confident of its rebirth . . .

Defeat—*Honor*

In 1820 the Duke of Wellington and his party had a shooting mishap. One of the party, a middle-aged lady, was shot accidentally in the leg by one of the duke's firings. The lady went into hysterics. Lady Shelley rushed to her and said, "Don't you see it's an honor to be shot by the great Duke of Wellington!"

And, similarly, I suppose it's an honor to be defeated by . . .

Defeat—*Landslide*

During the British general election of 1922, Sir Winston Churchill was convalescing from an appendicitis operation and could not campaign. In addition to this handicap, the Liberal Party, to which he belonged, had been badly split by dissenting factions. When the returns were in and he realized he was a private citizen again after many years in government, he shook his head sadly and murmured, "All of a sudden, I find myself without a seat, without a party, and without an appendix."

So although I still have an appendix, I find myself, like Churchill, part of an organization that is being disbanded and troops that are being dismissed . . .

Defeat—*Perseverance*

As the saying goes, we have lost a battle—but not necessarily the war. After the close of the Revolutionary War when General Nathanael Greene was asked by the French minister what the American strategy had been, Greene replied, "We fight, get beat, rise and fight again."

Defeat—*Sportsmanship*

I think we have all learned something from Winston Churchill's wit in adversity. I recall what Sarah Churchill wrote to her father when he was defeated in 1945: "You know it is ironically funny, you were saying, 'In war, resolution, in peace, goodwill, in victory, magnanimity, in defeat, defiance.' Well, you taught me the other night a great thing—in defeat, humor."

Defeat—*Support*

In the thirties and forties there was a much-traveled pitcher named Bobo Newsom. The big hurler was pitching for the St. Louis Browns at the time and was facing a hard-hitting Philadelphia Athletic lineup that was banging them back faster than Bobo could serve them up. The score mounted by leaps and bounds. By the seventh inning, the A's had a comfortable 15–0 lead, and Bobo came back to the dugout wearing a disgusted look on his broad face. "What's eating you, Bobo?" asked someone on the bench. "What do you think?" snorted the angry Newsom as he flung his glove aside. "How can a guy win ball games with this lousy club if they don't give him any runs?"

Well, *I* can't say in defeat that I wasn't given good support . . .

Demagogue—*Expedience*

John Wilkes, after haranguing the House of Commons for some hours, came to the Cheshire Cheese pub while Doctor Samuel Johnson was there and attempted then to remonstrate with the good Doctor. When Wilkes finished his tirade, Samuel Johnson observed, "This man has a pulse in his tongue."

And I characterize our demagogic friend as also sick . . .

Destination—*Ambition*

The scene was Edinburgh airport. A lass working for the British Board of Trade and assigned to quiz every thirtieth arriving passenger flipped open her pad. "What is the reason for your visit?" "Business, politics, winning an election," replied the pink-cheeked gentleman. "How long has your firm been in business?" "Since the time of Benjamin Disraeli." "What is your final destination?" "Number Ten Downing Street." Only then did she recognize Edward ("Ted") Heath, fifty-three, leader of the Conservative Party and aspirant prime minister.

And the Republican Party has been in business since before the Civil War and our final destination is the White House . . .

Determination—*Perseverance*

When a friend asked President Lincoln if he really expected to end the War Between the States during his administration, he replied, "Can't say, sir, can't say." "But, Mr. Lincoln, what do you mean to do?" "Peg away, sir, peg away. Keep pegging away!"

In a similar way we intend to carry on bit by bit—unending in our endeavor . . .

Determination—*Resolution*

Long after Andrew Jackson died someone asked Alfred, an old servant of Jackson's, if he thought his master would get into heaven on Judgment Day. Alfred knew his man. "If General Jackson takes it into his head to git to heaven," he said, "who's gwine to keep him out?"

Well, such is the determination of our next speaker, who has succeeded in everything he has set his mind to . . .

Dictator—*Humanity*

In 1939 English novelist Virginia Woolf called out to her husband, who was working in their garden, "Come listen—Hitler is on the wireless." Her husband replied, "I shan't come. I'm busy planting iris and they will be flowering long after he is dead."

Dilemma—*Mess*

One afternoon, when former catcher Joe Garagiola was with the Cardinals, a Pirate pitcher named Rip Sewell tried to knock him down. Garagiola promptly laid the next pitch down the first-base line and tried to climb up Sewell's back with his spikes. But the pitcher threw a block at Joe that kicked him right into the Pirates' dugout. "Next thing I knew," says Joe, "one Pirate had me by one leg, another by the other leg, and somebody was saying, 'Make a wish.'"

Well, I can assure you that, caught between the choices I've told you about, I myself was making a wish . . .

Dinner—*Communication*

Alice Roosevelt Longworth in the role of one of Washington's leading hostesses, had the ability to get people to mingle easily at gatherings. One evening, however, she faced a real challenge: to get Calvin Coolidge to loosen up and talk a bit. Seated next to him during the meal, she said to Coolidge, after numerous attempts to make him talk, "I guess going to all these parties must bore you. Why do you go?" "Well," said Silent Cal, "a man has to eat somewhere."

And I guess that explains the origin of political banquets . . .

Dinner—*Food*

I want to thank those who made this dinner such a success. I find myself agreeing with what a British statesman once said. Joseph Chamberlain was a gourmet. When a reporter asked him how a man of affairs could take so much interest in food, he replied, "So many pleasures of life are illusionary, but a good dinner is a reality."

Diplomacy—*Compromise*

When Prime Minister Harold Macmillan was British Resident Minister in Algeria during World War II, he was called upon to settle a dispute between British and American officers in the Allied mess. The Americans wanted drinks served before meals, the British after. Macmillan's solution was worthy of Solomon. "Henceforth," he said, "we will all drink before meals in deference to the Americans, and we will all drink after dinner in deference to the British."

And in the spirit of such a happy compromise we have decided to extend invitations to both groups . . .

Direct—*Salesmanship*

When France indicated its intention to help the American colonies win their independence, John Paul Jones, the newly commissioned American naval officer, sailed to Le Havre in the hopes of being given three battle sloops. Letter after letter Jones wrote to King Louis XVI asking for the ships, but there was no answer from Versailles. One day while reading a copy of *Poor Richard's Almanac,* which Benjamin Franklin had given him, he came across the saying "Never send a letter when you can go in person." Jones did go in person to Versailles and Louis XVI outfitted him with the three sloops. In recognition of Franklin's advice Jones named his flagship *Le Bonhomme Richard.* John Paul Jones learned to take matters in his own hands and the rest is history. Even in our day, this piece of homely wisdom has its place . . .

Direction—*Objective*

Of all our Presidents, none has been so avid and eager a golfer as Dwight D. Eisenhower. At every opportunity he would go out to the links. One time Bob Hope was playing with the President and noticed that Eisenhower kept looking at his wrist. "Why do you keep looking at your watch?" he asked the President. "This isn't a watch," replied Ike. "It's a compass!"

Similarly, I think it is time we take some bearings . . .

Disagreement—*Respect*

It is no secret that I disagree with much of what the speaker stands for. I am reminded of what the famous biographer James Boswell once said. He did not agree with the agnostic theories of his fellow Scotsman David Hume. On one visit to Edinburgh, Boswell told the philosopher, "How much better are you than your books!"

And how much better I like the speaker than some of his statements . . .

Discipline—*Success*

The difference between success and mediocrity is not so much talent as training and mental discipline. A reporter visited Mark Twain's haunts in Hannibal, Missouri, some years ago in order to gather material for an in-depth profile of the famous man. He found one crony who discounted the glory and fame of his erstwhile school chum. "Shucks," he said, "I knew as many stories as Sam Clemens. He just writ them down."

Doctorate—*Title*

I'm afraid that at home I am regarded much as the great physicist Robert A. Millikan was regarded in his household. His wife happened to pass through the hall of their home in time to hear the maid answer the telephone. "Yes," Mrs. Millikan overheard, "this is where Dr. Millikan lives, but he's not the kind of doctor that does anybody any good."

Similarly, I'm not the kind of doctor who does anyone any good . . .

Economy—*Business*

Back in 1962 President John F. Kennedy was exchanging pleasantries with a conservative industrialist at the White House. "You know," mused the Chief Executive, "if I weren't President, I'd be buying stocks now." "Yes," said the businessman. "And if you weren't President, I'd be buying them, too."

And if we today had different leadership at the helm, I'd have a lot more confidence . . .

Economy—*Judgment*

Dining with Prime Minister William Pitt at 10 Downing Street, Edmund Burke strove to make Pitt understand how critical the national economic situation was. Pitt made light of the danger, saying, "This country and this constitution are safe to the day of judgment." "Yes," replied Burke, "but 'tis the day of 'no judgment' that I am afraid of."

So today are we afraid of a national administration that exercises no judgment in monetary policy—government leaders who exercise no prudence but push the country toward economic disaster.

Education—*Bored*

No truly educated man can become bored. He can always call upon his mental resources. Once at a particularly dull academic meeting a fellow guest remarked sympathetically to Thomas Edison, "I am afraid you are terribly bored, Mr. Edison." "Oh, no," replied Edison, pleasantly. "On occasions like this I retire to the back of my mind, and there I am happy."

Education—*Campaign*

As we launch this drive today I think of a reply once made to Good Queen Bess in the sixteenth century. Queen Elizabeth had noted the presence of one of her favorite courtiers, Sir Walter Mildmay, who had been missing from court for some time. "Sir Walter," she said, "where have you been?" Mildmay, who had been away establishing Emmanuel College at Cambridge, replied, "Madam, I have been away planting an acorn. And when it becomes an oak, God only knoweth what it will amount to."

Education—*Service*

Horace Mann has been called America's greatest educator. A brilliant lawyer, he entered politics and became president of the Massachusetts State Senate. A man of vision, he saw the vast possibilities which lay in developing the public education system of the nation. His pleas for education brought results; Massachusetts created a State Board of Education. No outstanding man could be found for the job of first secretary of the Board. Despite the fact that Mann had such brilliant prospects for a political career, which many thought would lead to the presidency, Mann, to the astonishment of all, gave up his political career and his lucrative law practice to take the job of first secretary of the Board of Education. Mann's reply to those who said that the position was a step down, unworthy of a man of his stature, was "If the title is not sufficiently honorable, then it is clearly left to me to elevate it; and I had rather be creditor than debtor to the title."

In just such a way our speaker has ennobled his position. He has brought to the title a new meaning and dignity . . .

Education—*University*

Aristotle, pupil of Plato and tutor of Alexander the Great, was once questioned by a citizen on the value of education. "What," asked the questioner, "is the difference between an educated and an uneducated man?" "The same difference," Aristotle replied, "as between being alive and being dead."

We have here an alive university that meets the needs of a modern diversified society . . .

₸

The purpose of a university education is not to cram facts but to expose the mind to a spectrum of mental and philosophical challenges. A person once sarcastically asked Robert M. Hutchins, former president of the University of Chicago, if Communism was still being taught at the university. "Yes," replied Hutchins, "and cancer at the medical school."

Ending—*Success*

Movie mogul Sam Goldwyn once told writer Dorothy Parker, "You and your wisecracks. I told you, there's no money in wisecracks. People want a happy ending."

"I know this will come as a shock to you, Mr. Goldwyn, but in all history, which has held billions and billions of human beings, not a single one ever had a happy ending," observed the writer.

However, whatever our ultimate conclusion, we have seen one happy ending today . . .

Endorsement—*Uncomfortable*

In the 1940s Vito Marcantonio, the Communist-leaning New York City Congressman, was a tough man to deal with in debate. Once, in an exchange with Texas Congressman Milton West on the floor or the House, Marcantonio threatened to come to Texas in the next campaign. "I'd defeat you for sure," yelled Vito.

"Having you fight me would be a big help," retorted West.

"Oh, I wouldn't fight you," said the Red-tainted Marcantonio, "I'd endorse you."

Well, I myself am feeling pretty uncomfortable with some of the groups who are supporting, for the wrong reasons, some of the objectives I am . . .

Energy—*Industry*

In 1776 James Boswell visited Matthew Boulton, the partner of James Watt, the inventor and builder of steam engines. Boulton proclaimed to Boswell, "I sell here, sir, what all the world desires to have—power."

Today the nation needs more and fuller sources of power if we are to expand our economy and provide for an abundant future . . .

Enterprise—*Failure*

Over a hundred years ago when Gail Borden, American pioneer and inventor, was crossing the Atlantic from England, two children on board died because the milk was contaminated. He began to dream of a way to make milk safe for shipboard use. He eventually discovered a way through a principle called "condensed milk." When Gail Borden died, his gravestone carried this epitaph: "I tried and failed. I tried again and again and succeeded."

The secret of business success is the combination of imagination and enterprise . . .

Enthusiasm—*Lip Service*

It is not enough just to carry out your assignment, you have to believe in what you're saying. It reminds me of what Mark Twain once said. Twain's habit of swearing was upsetting to his wife, who tried her best to cure him of it. One day, while shaving, he cut himself. He recited his entire vocabulary and when he was finished, his wife, hoping to shock him, repeated every word he had said. Twain stunned her by saying calmly, "You have the words, dear, but you don't know the tune."

Error—*God*

The German Catholic prelate Cardinal von Faulhaber of Munich once had a conversation with the physicist Albert Einstein.

"Cardinal von Faulhaber," Einstein remarked, "I respect religion, but I believe in mathematics. Probably it is the other way around with you."

"You are mistaken," the Cardinal replied. "To me, both are merely different expressions of the same divine exactness."

"But, your Eminence, what would you say if mathematical science should someday come to conclusions directly contradictory to religious beliefs?"

"Oh," answered the Cardinal, "I have the highest respect for the competence of mathematicians. I am sure they would never rest until they discovered their mistake."

And similarly I have great respect for our friends on the other side and I am confident they will eventually discover the error of their ways.

Ethics—*Politics*

Too many politicians think ethics are irrelevant to politics. In 1959 during an interview a reporter asked British Prime Minister Harold Macmillan, "Sir, what do you think is the real meaning of life?" "Good God," replied Macmillan, "if you want to know the meaning of life, see your Archbishop, don't ask a politician."

Example—*Enlightenment*

When Benjamin Franklin wished to interest the people of Philadelphia in street lighting, he didn't try to persuade them by talking about it—instead, he hung a beautiful lantern on a long bracket before his own door. Then he kept the glass brightly polished, and carefully and religiously lit the wick every evening at the approach of dusk. People wandering about on the dark street saw Franklin's light a long way off and came under the influence of its friendly glow with grateful hearts. It wasn't long before Franklin's neighbors began placing lights in brackets before their homes, and soon the entire city awoke to the value of street lighting and took up the matter with interest and enthusiasm.

Excellence—*Artist*

A young songwriter was once putting down Irving Berlin as being overrated. "Hell," he said, " 'All Alone by the Telephone'—what's that? Anybody could write that." "Yes," said Oscar Hammerstein, "anybody could, but Irving Berlin did."

And the point is that nobody but our speaker could have . . .

Excellence—*Award*

Some people may wonder why it is necessary to give awards. I think the best answer to that question was given by the great German mathematician Karl Gustav Jacobi. Doctor Jacobi, a giant in the development of arithmetic theory, was asked one day why he decided to spend his life at work in such an abstract and aesthetic realm. "For the honor of the human spirit," he replied.

Similarly, that is why we pay tribute to excellence. All excellence honors the human spirit.

Excellence—*Beauty*

In old age, Pierre Auguste Renoir, the great French painter, suffered from arthritis, which twisted and cramped his hands. Henri Matisse, his artist friend, watched sadly while Renoir, grasping a brush with only his fingertips, continued to paint, even though each movement caused stabbing pain.

One day, Matisse asked Renoir why he persisted in painting at the expense of such torture.

Renoir replied, "The pain passes, but the beauty remains."

Well, whatever sacrifice it has meant, we can today see the enduring beauty . . .

Excellence—*Compensation*

Catherine II was treating her court to concerts by Catterina Gabrielli, the celebrated Italian soprano. The Russian Empress had asked the artist to come to St. Petersburg without stating any definite price. Gabrielli determined, however, that a royal patron should be royally charged. When at the end of the season Catherine asked the entertainer what she was to be paid for her singing, she replied, "Five thousand ducats."

"Five thousand ducats!" the empress exclaimed. "Why, not one of my field marshals is paid as much as that."

"Well, then," retorted Gabrielli, "Your Majesty had better get one of your field marshals to sing for you."

Excellence—*Competition*

Brendan Gill, of *The New Yorker*, during an interview was asked what was the secret of the magazine's unique success. Gill replied, "It was friction. Friction between Harold Ross, positive and Harold Ross, negative."

In a similar sense, we could say the success of the accomplishment we honor today has also been the result of friction . . .

Excellence—*Introduction*

The eloquent introduction reminds me of a remark once made by Oscar Levant. When the American composer George Gershwin died, a man of sentiment combined with musical aspirations wrote an elegy in his honor. He sought out Oscar Levant, who reluctantly granted him a hearing. Eagerly the man played the piano piece, and then turned expectantly toward Levant, seeking approbation. "I think it would have been better," Levant said, "if you had died and Gershwin had written the elegy."

Similarly, it would have been better if I had given the introduction, then you could have enjoyed a brilliant speech . . .

Excellence—*Passive*

One Thanksgiving afternoon some years ago, sleepy Jim Crowley, former Notre Dame ace and coach of Fordham's football team, sat huddled in misery on the sidelines, watching a New York University eleven make monkeys of his powerful Rams. The clever passing combination of Buell and Dunney was bewildering Fordham defense. At last, Crowley lost patience with the situation. Inspecting his bench, his eyes lit on an eager and ambitious sophomore back. Heck, thought Crowley to himself, this kid couldn't do worse against that pair than the guys in there. He called the green youngster to his side and gave him careful instructions. "Now listen," he said, "I want you to get in there and just keep your eye on Dunney. Do you understand? Never mind where the ball is, or who's got it. You just keep your eye on Dunney. Now get out there!" The sophomore nodded and leaped into the fray. As luck would have it, his presence on the field seemed to make no difference. The Buell to Dunney passing combination continued on its merry way and the Violets scored again. Crowley blew his top. "Go in there," he barked to his regular halfback, "and tell that kid to come out!" When the sophomore returned to the bench, Crowley was there to greet him. "What do you think you were doing out there?" he demanded angrily. "Didn't I tell you to watch Dunney?" "Oh, yes, sir," replied the green young kid, "and I did every minute. Boy, is he a fantastic player!"

And from the some-time vantage point of the opposition we have watched our guest of honor—and we can tell you—he is fantastic . . .

Excellence—*Popular*

Once Prime Minister Lloyd George, while traveling through Wales, was obliged to stop overnight in a little town. He could find no hotel and so he knocked at the door of a large brick building, and said to the man who answered, "Can you put me up for the night?"

The man said, "This is an insane asylum."

"Well," said Lloyd George, "I must sleep somewhere; can't you take care of me? I am David Lloyd George."

Replied the man, "I say, my dear fellow, we have five Lloyd Georges here already, but I suppose there is always room for a sixth."

And so there is always room for another . . .

Excellence—*Portrait*

After looking at this picture, I can understand the remark of Charles V, the Holy Roman Emperor, when he was shown his portrait by Titian. "Now that I have been painted by the best," he declared, "I never want another picture made."

Excellence—*Replacement*

As I consider the merits of the one whom I follow, my thoughts turn to the words of Thomas Jefferson. When Benjamin Franklin, who had served brilliantly as American ambassador, left France, Thomas Jefferson, who followed Franklin in the post, was received by the Comte de Vergennes.

"You replace Dr. Franklin?" inquired the French count.

"No one can ever replace Franklin," replied Jefferson. "I merely succeed him."

Excuse—*Party*

When friends get together one hardly needs much of an excuse to uncork a bottle. The best precedent for that is the action by one of our first Chief Justices of the Supreme Court—John Marshall. The Justices, in rainy weather, were accustomed to meet in an oak-paneled conference room in the Capitol and have a few hot-buttered rum toddies in front of the fireplace. On one sunny day as the Justices sat down for the Friday morning voting session Chief Justice Marshall called for rum and then raised his glass. "Gentlemen, this court has jurisdiction over most of this entire continent," he said. "Somewhere it is raining; therefore, henceforth, we shall begin all of our sessions with similar fortification."

Executive—*Efficiency*

Once young Benjamin Franklin, growing up in Boston, was curiously watching his father storing away for the winter their provisions which had been salted for long keeping. "I think, Father," said Benjamin, "if you were to say grace over the whole cask you would save a lot of time each evening."

It was that sense of economy that led Franklin to conceive of so many inventions. Today we must find a way to improve our method . . .

Executive—*Follow-through*

Once at the Ford Motor Company an ambitious young employee sought out Henry Ford and asked him, "How can I make my life a success?" Mr. Ford's answer was simply, "When you start a thing finish it."

And with Henry Ford, I would say the essential requisite for the makings of a top executive is the ability to follow through . . .

Executive—*Implementation*

In January 1953 outgoing President Truman was preparing the transition to President-elect Dwight David Eisenhower. While organizing the packing of his own effects and files in the Oval Office, he said to an aide, "Poor Ike—he'll sit right here and he'll say 'Do this, do that,' and nothing will happen. It won't be like the army. He'll find it very frustrating."

Executive—*Mess*

The only way I can describe the managerial record is to appropriate a saying of the late Chicago Mayor Dick Daley. Describing events at the riotous 1968 Democratic Convention, he told a press conference, "The police are not here to create disorder. They are here to preserve disorder."

Executive—*Personnel*

Any lobbyist will tell you that the secret of getting things done in Washington is knowing all the secretaries. But this holds true in any business. Never put yourself above anybody. One of the most popular Congressmen ever was Private John Allen of Tupelo, Mississippi. He always carried the title "Private" because of the way he was elected in 1884. His principal opponent was General Tucker of the Army of the Confederacy, in which Allen had served as a private. In one memorable debate, the General contrasted his high rank with John Allen's. "Yes, sir," replied Allen, "I admit I was only a private. In fact, I was a sentry who stood guard over the general when he slept. And now all you fellows who were generals and had privates standing guard over you, vote for General Tucker. But all you boys who were privates and stood guard over the generals, vote for Private John Allen." They did, and he served for the next sixteen years.

Executive—*Unconstitutional*

In 1832 Andrew Jackson was writing a veto message, overruling an act of Congress which was to establish a national bank. Jackson, in his veto, said that the act was unconstitutional. His secretary said, "You can't make that statement because a similar act has been before the Supreme Court and its constitutionality has been upheld by the Supreme Court. You are sworn to uphold the Constitution." Andy Jackson replied, "I am sworn to uphold the Constitution as Andy Jackson understands it and interprets it."

And it looks like the present Chief Executive is taking a leaf from Andy Jackson's book . . .

Exit—*Speaker*

When West Point had that unforgettable juggernaut which for three years rolled over everything in sight, the brightest star of that undefeated gridiron powerhouse was Doc Blanchard, who in his day was the most feared football player in the land. A bone-crushing fullback, he was hailed as one of the greatest in history. When Blanchard hit a rival line it was said that that particular spot of earth trembled.

Now a courageous Navy team was the victim. A midshipman kicked off and Glenn Davis, Blanchard's touchdown twin, ran the ball back to Navy's 30-yard line. After the huddle as the Army players lined up for the next play, one of Army's giant tackles looked up at his Navy opponent and snapped: "Look, pal, Doc Blanchard is coming through this spot on the next play. I don't know what you're going to do, but I'm getting the hell out of here!"

Well, knowing the powerful speaker who is next on the program, I'm going to clear out . . .

Expediency—*Betrayal*

I can condone compromise—I can even understand expedience—but I cannot see the advantage in the adoption of a program that betrays everything we have ever stood for—a program that will gain us little. It recalls the circumstances in which Sir Thomas More, the lord chancellor, was executed in 1535. He was convicted by his protégé Richard Richards, who gave perjured testimony against More—the perjurer then became attorney-general for Wales. After Richards's false testimony More looked at him and said, "I know it might profit you to gain a whole nation for the price of a soul—but for Wales?"

Expediency—*Morality*

Sir Edward Grey, British Foreign Secretary in World War I, was once asked by a young reporter, "Sir, do you find it difficult as foreign secretary to reconcile your private morality with your public positions?" "Well, you see," Sir Edward said, after a long pause, "I have discovered that to do the right thing is generally the right thing to do."

Similarly, we should ask ourselves not what is the most expedient thing to do, but what is the right thing.

Expense—*Cost*

In my commitment to underwrite the expenses I want you to know that I am only going to reimburse on those bills that are absolutely essential. I recall an incident in 1958 when it was well known that J.F.K. would seek the Democratic nomination for President. He said to the members of the Gridiron Club, "I have just received the following wire from my generous Daddy—'Dear Jack—Don't buy a single vote more than necessary. I'll be damned if I am going to pay for a landslide.'"

Experience—*Life*

When the motto of the Hanover Club of Göttingen, to which as a student he had belonged, was quoted to him as applicable to his own life, Prussian statesman Otto von Bismarck reflected, "Yes, 'No Steps Backwards,' but a good many zigzags."

And in that catalogue of successes listed in that introduction, there have been many zigzags . . .

Experience—*Retirement*

When I think of my experience in the past years, I am reminded of one of the last remarks of Sir Winston Churchill. The feeble dying ninety-year-old clasped the hand of his good American friend Kay Halle, whom he was seeing for the last time, and said, "It was a grand journey worth taking—once."

Expert—*Advice*

John McGraw, who won ten pennants as manager of the New York Giants, was a soft touch for every panhandler in town. One day, one of the characters who used to hit McGraw regularly for a handout buttonholed the famous manager. "How about slipping me a buck for coffee?" he pleaded. McGraw was in a dark mood that day and turned on the beggar with a scowl. "A buck for a cup of coffee?" he snapped. "Are you out of your mind?" "Look, Mr. McGraw," replied the bum patiently, "do I tell you how to manage a ball club? Well, then, don't tell me how to panhandle!"

Expert—*Audience*

As I look at this audience, I am reminded of the time Billie Burke, the famous actress, while enjoying a transatlantic ocean trip noticed that a gentleman at the next table was suffering from a bad cold. "Are you very uncomfortable?" she asked sympathetically. The man nodded. "I'll tell you just what to do for it," she offered. "Go back to your stateroom and drink lots of orange juice. Take five aspirin tablets. Cover yourself with all the blankets you can find. Sweat the cold out. I know just what I am talking about. I am Billie Burke of Hollywood." The man smiled warmly, and introduced himself in return. "Thanks," he said, "I am Dr. Mayo, of the Mayo Clinic."

Thus, I am a little hesitant about speaking with so many experts in the audience . . .

Expertise—*Unfamiliar*
When British Parliamentarian Charles James Fox wrote a biography of James II, the English essayist Hazlitt commented, "I don't blame Fox for writing a mediocre history of King James. I blame him for having written a history at all. It wasn't his business to write history."

Similarly, our learned public servant is a very clever fellow, but in this field he is out of his depth . . .

Explanation—*Translation*
The New York Giants and the Chicago White Sox made a worldwide tour about sixty-five years ago and the two teams played exhibitions in all the capitals of Europe. It fell to none other than tough, hard-boiled John McGraw to act as guide, interpreter, and information agent when the two clubs reached London. His Majesty, King George V, attended the game and McGraw sat in the box with the king to help explain what went on on the field. A White Sox player laid down a bunt with a man on base and the runner on first went to second as the put-out was made at first base. "That's called a sacrifice, Your Majesty," said McGraw graciously. "We call it a sacrifice because the batter gave himself up for the other man so he could advance from first to second base." There were several moments of heavy silence in the royal box and McGraw was embarrassed to think that his explanation had failed to be understood. Then the king cleared his throat. "I say," he said, "that was rawther sporting of the chap."

You see, it is not always easy to explain the customs and institutions of a culture to a person who is unfamiliar . . .

Extremism—*Injustice*
During the French Revolution many of the liberty-loving moderates were executed by the radicals. One of these was the beautiful and talented Madame Roland. On her way to her execution in a donkey cart during the Terror, she had the cart stop in front of a

colossal statue of Liberty and said to the onlookers, "O Liberty! How many crimes are committed in thy name!"

Facade—*Superficial*

We live in a world where politicians preen themselves. It reminds me of the time Ralph Waldo Emerson first heard abolitionist Wendell Phillips speak. He wrote in his journal: "The first discovery I made of Phillips was that while I admired his eloquence, I had not the faintest wish to meet the man. He had only a platform existence, and no personality."

Today all too many of our media and public figures are plastic, without depth or texture.

Facts—*Emotion*

With all the emotion that has been engendered on this subject, I think it wise to follow the advice of Benjamin Franklin. The town of Franklin, Massachusetts, which was named for him, sent a letter to the aged doctor in Philadelphia saying, "We have named our town after you and we should like a donation of a sum of money from you in order that we may put a bell in the town hall steeple."

Dr. Franklin wrote back, "I am very much honored, very glad indeed to send you a sum of money, only don't buy a bell with it. Buy a public library because I have always preferred sense to sound."

Facts—*Reality*

In 1961 Oklahoma's powerful Senator Bob Kerr asked President Kennedy if he could have a few minutes of his time. Kerr was upset that J.F.K. was going to veto the recently passed bill to bar the importation of zinc. Kerr was strongly supported by zinc manufacturers in western Oklahoma. Kennedy received him at the Oval Office with aide Mike Feldman and Ted Sorensen and said, "Bob, I'm sorry but it's a bad bill."

"Mr. President, could I speak to you privately? There are a few things you may not understand about the legislation."

"Sure, Bob, but it's not going to change my mind. I've been

briefed pretty thoroughly by Ted and Mike."

When Sorensen and Feldman left the room, Kerr drawled, "Mr. President, you are my leader and I will abide by your decision."

"Bob, I appreciate that."

"But, Mr. President, my people were pretty mad when Ike vetoed that same bill, and I will have to go back to Oklahoma and spend full-time defending your action."

"I really appreciate that."

"But, Mr. President, you understand that that means that if I'm away in Oklahoma, your tax bill, which lies in the Finance Committee which I chair, will never come to the floor."

"Bob, this is the first time anyone really explained the zinc bill to me—I'll sign it."

Well, like Bob Kerr, I think it is the time to explain the facts of life . . .

Failure—*Determination*

I do not look upon this development as a defeat. For even in our defeat we have discovered new things about ourselves. It reminds me of the time Thomas Edison was mocked for trying unsuccessfully some twelve hundred materials for the filament of his great dream, the incandescent light bulb. "You have failed twelve hundred times," said a regimented thinker of that day. "I have not failed," countered Edison. "I have discovered twelve hundred materials that won't work."

Fame—*Fleeting*

A small lad came up to President Hoover just after he had left the White House and asked for his autograph. When the former President graciously complied, the little fellow said, "Would you mind signing it again, further down?" "All right," said Mr. Hoover, and did so. Then he asked, "But why twice?" "Because," was the young businessman's answer, "with two of yours I can get one of Babe Ruth's."

Well, today I can report that no one is seeking my autograph . . .

Familiarity—*Communication*

When Alfred Lunt and Lynn Fontanne, a notably devoted husband and wife, started rehearsing *At Mrs. Bean's,* a play in which it was necessary for Miss Fontanne to strike Mr. Lunt in the face, she found she couldn't hit him. She pulled her hand back and let go—and then stopped dead before she struck. Her husband begged her to do it, but after thirty minutes she still couldn't. Finally, Mr. Lunt shouted, "For God's sake, Lynn, you're the lousiest actress I've ever played opposite!" The Fontanne hand made a direct hit. Mr. Lunt yelped with pain, then grinned. But when they put on the show he had to whisper, "You know you're lousy, dear," each time before she would hit him.

Well, we all know that it is sometimes hardest to communicate with those we best know and love . . .

Family—*Fame*

The one we honor today comes from a noted family. He might say, if he were less modest, what British actress Lynn Redgrave said when she was asked by a BBC interviewer why she and her sister Vanessa chose the acting profession like their father, Sir Michael Redgrave. Said Lynn, "When we were young, we decided to follow in our father's footlights."

Family—*Home*

A Viennese woman once asked Sigmund Freud, "How early should I begin the education of my child?" "When will your child be born?" Freud asked. "Born?" she exclaimed. "Why, he is already five years old!" "My goodness, woman," the famous psychoanalyst cried, "don't stand there talking to me—hurry home! You have already wasted the five best years!"

Indeed, it is the home and love in early years more than any school that shape the growth of the mind . . .

Family—*Hurt*

The familiar song echoes "You always hurt the one you love." The axiom recalls to me an incident in the life of General George Patton. In 1940 my father, Judge Samuel Hamilton Humes, was in charge of getting a speaker for the Saturday Exercises in observance of Armistice Day at Hill School, a boys' preparatory school in Pennsylvania. My father, an alumnus, thought Patton, then a colonel, would deliver an inspiring message. The headmaster, Dr. James Wendell, demurred.

"Sam," he argued, "George is a fine man but he has a reputation for salty talk—perhaps not the right thing for impressionable young ears."

Patton, whose son George, III, was a senior at the school, assured my father, "Sam, I know how to talk to young men. Don't worry."

Well, Patton was true to his word. He gave an eloquent oration on duty, honor, and country. After lunch they all went out to watch Hill play its traditional rival, Lawrenceville, in football. In the last minute of the game, with Lawrenceville leading 6–0, the Hill quarterback threw a long pass. Young George Patton, an end, was waiting on the goal line. He caught it then dropped it.

His father, sitting next to my father, stormed onto the field using all the expurgated phrases of Anglo-Saxon known to man, chewing out his own son. With his own family he forgot his manners.

Family—*Motive*

Thomas Erskine, the British barrister who became lord chancellor, became famous with his first case. The young man eloquently argued before the feared Lord Mansfield. He even had the boldness to remind the esteemed judge of a few obscure legal points. The result was acquittal for his client. Acclaimed by his colleagues for his magnificent presentation, he was asked how he had the courage to speak so bluntly to Lord Mansfield. His answer became legendary: "Because I thought I heard my little ones pulling at my barrister's gown saying, 'Now, Father, now is the time to give us bread.'"

Family—*Winner*

During the course of his travels one summer, Frank Leahy, coach of the all-powerful Notre Dame footballers, ran into an old friend who had not seen him in some time. "Hey, Frank," said the friend, "understand you're married now." "That's right," answered Frank. "How many children do you have?" In answer, Leahy held up his right hand with all fingers spread. The friend whistled, then shook his head. "Five?" he cried in astonishment. Then he grinned. "But why should I be surprised? You never were the guy to hold down the score!"

Well, our next speaker as a father of five has racked up . . .

Father—*Children*

Man has no greater responsibility than that of fatherhood. Once at the close of the sixteenth century, King Henry IV of France was interrupted in his royal chamber by the Spanish ambassador. The envoy found the French king playing the part of horse while his young son rode atop. Though the diplomat was astonished, the king was matter of fact. "You are a father too, Señor Ambassador. So we will finish our ride."

Feminism—*Wife*

When the Queen of Sweden interceded with her husband on behalf of some citizens who had suffered under recent Court edicts she flung herself at his feet, begging for some compassion for his subjects. Charles XI answered, "Madam, we took you in order to have children, not to get advice."

Well, today, things fortunately are different . . .

Feminism—*Women*

Napoleon Bonaparte said to Madame de Condorcet, the widow of the philosopher, who was a great female politician and a woman of real talent, "I do not like women who meddle with politics." Madame de Condorcet instantly replied, "Ah, *mon général,* as long as you men take a fancy to cut off our heads now and then, we are interested in knowing why you do it."

Today women are increasingly asking more questions . . .

Flattery—*Introduction*

My wife remarked the other day that the most difficult thing in the world to do is to accept a compliment gracefully. I face this difficulty now—on the heels of your president's introduction. I am not going to ignore it in the hope of leaving the impression that I am used to this sort of tribute. I am going to follow the example of the eighteenth-century English philosopher Samuel Johnson, who was called to the king's library for an interview and returned to tell his friends that the king had complimented him highly on his eloquence. "What did you reply to the king?" asked the friends. "Why," said Samuel Johnson, "I took him at his word. Who am I to bandy civilities with my sovereign?"

And who am I to bandy civilities with the president of this graduating class? I have listened with exceeding care to every word he said, and I am satisfied with his presentation to the last detail.

Flattery—*Introduction*

Once in a debate in the House of Representatives, a Congressman addressed a speech in a complimentary vein to the irascible John Randolph of Virginia. At the conclusion, a seat-mate said to him, "Aren't you going to answer?" "Answer, sir," said Randolph, "that speech wasn't made to be answered."

And likewise that introduction you just heard wasn't made to be answered . . .

Form—*Beauty*

I remember the time a pretty young tennis star appeared on one of Groucho Marx's television shows and spoke about her training for an upcoming tournament. "I need to improve my form and speed," she said. "If your form improves," Groucho replied archly, "you are going to need all the speed you can muster."

In this regard our young friend's form needs no improvement . . .

Fund Raising—*Conditional*

Robert Falcon Scott, the explorer, applied to David Lloyd George for assistance in the financing of his last, fatal South Pole expedition. The then chancellor of the exchequer referred him to a certain wealthy man, also of some prominence in the political scene. "How did you succeed?" asked Lloyd George when the explorer again called on him. "He gave me a thousand pounds" was the reply, "but he has undertaken to raise twenty thousand pounds if I can persuade you to come with me, and a million if I manage to leave you there."

Well, if we promised to leave a certain party on the moon, I'm sure we'd have no trouble raising . . .

Future—*Children*

Once Adlai Stevenson noticed children in the audiences during his presidential campaign appearances, he would ask, "How many children would like to be a candidate for the presidency of the United States?" Almost all of the kids would raise their hands. Then Stevenson would ask, "And how many candidates for the presidency of the United States would like to be children again?" At that point he would raise his own hand.

Well, we can't be children again but at least we can make it possible for more children to have the opportunities for real fun and play . . .

Future—*Legacy*

On his deathbed Governor James Stephen Hogg of Texas requested that no monument be placed at his grave; but that instead there be planted, "at my head a pecan tree, and at my feet an old-fashioned walnut, and when these trees shall bear, let the pecans and walnuts be given out among the Plains people of Texas, so that they may plant them and make Texas a land of trees."

Today we also have an opportunity to provide a legacy . . .

Future—*Planning*

We owe a duty to our children and grandchildren to begin planning now. We also can learn from what Henry Clay once did. Senator Clay was driving in a stagecoach from Washington to Kentucky. A friend asked Clay if he was supporting his American plan for internal improvements, such as roads and canals. At the next stop, Clay got out of the coach and put his ear down to the ground, and told his friend to do likewise. When his companion claimed he didn't hear anything, Clay replied, "I do . . . I hear the tread of the unborn thousands."

Future—*Problem*

I know it is coming. I can't exactly see in what shape or form, but I know, just like the time Roy Sievers faced Herb Score. In his first two years with the Indians, Herb Score threw just about as fast as anyone who ever lived. One day Roy Sievers stepped in against him, and it was buzz, buzz, buzz—three quick strikes. Roy strolled to the dugout, politely put his bat into the rack, and sat down. "He threw me the radio ball," he announced. "Radio ball?" asked Chuck Stobbs. "That's right," said Sievers. "You can hear it, but you can't see it."

Well, from the things I am hearing, I can tell you . . .

Generosity—*Host*

William M. Evarts was Secretary of State for Rutherford B. Hayes, whose wife, nicknamed "Lemonade Lucy," presided over a "dry" White House. Evarts was a bibulous, but loyal minister. He was once asked how he liked the state dinners. "Great," he exalted, "the water flows like champagne."

Well, here at least the wine is flowing like water . . .

Genius—*Greatness*

In 1882 Oscar Wilde came to America for the first time to undertake a lecture tour. As he landed at New York, a customs official asked him if he had anything to declare. "No," said Wilde, "I have nothing to declare"—and he paused— "except my genius."

Well, our speaker does not have to declare his genius, his works and contributions speak for themselves . . .

Genius—*Talent*

A young composer once came to Mozart for advice on how to develop his talents. "Begin writing simple things first," Mozart told him. "Write songs, for example." "But you composed symphonies when you were only a child!" the young man exclaimed. "Oh," Mozart answered, "but I did not go to anybody to find out how to become a composer."

Well, our speaker today is a born salesman . . .

Gentlemanly—*Fairness*

Just because we are rivals and competitors doesn't mean we can't act like gentlemen. I remember the time Ambassador Henry Cabot Lodge, in some annoyance, inquired why "the gentleman" kept demanding the floor at the United Nations.

"I am not a gentlemen, I am representative of the Soviet Union here," replied the Soviet delegate Tsaropkin. Murmured Lodge, "The two are not necessarily mutually exclusive."

Similarly, I don't think it makes good sense to take an ungentlemanly attitude . . .

God—*Atheism*

At the final service of one of evangelist Dwight Moody's campaigns, an usher handed him a note as he entered the auditorium. Supposing it to be an announcement, Moody quieted the large audience and prepared to read the notice. He opened it to find a single word, "Fool." But the eloquent preacher was equal to the occasion. Said he, "This is most unusual. I have just been handed a message which consists of but one word—the word 'fool.' I repeat, this is most unusual. I have often heard of those who have written letters and forgotten to sign their names, but this is the first time I have ever heard of anyone who signed his name and forgot to write the letter!" And taking advantage of the situation,

Moody promptly changed his sermon to the text "The fool hath said in his heart, there is no God."

God—*Church*

When John C. Calhoun was a Senator he offered to put up any visiting South Carolinian in his Washington home. There was one condition: the guest had to attend the family prayer session. When one demurred, Calhoun said to his servant, "Saddle that man's horse and see that he goes."

Calhoun was not afraid to alienate a constituent by taking a strong spiritual stand . . .

God—*Faith*

When Professor Charles William Eliot was president of Harvard University he had occasion to dedicate a new hall of philosophy and searched for an appropriate inscription to place above its entrance. He called his faculty members together and after much deliberation they suggested the well-known Greek maxim "Man is the measure of all things." With that they adjourned for their summer vacation. When school reopened in the fall, they were surprised to find that the president had decided upon his own inscription. Instead of "Man is the measure of all things" he had seen fit to have inscribed, "What is man that Thou art mindful of him?"

And so we ask, What is God's plan for us? . . .

God—*Medicine*

Lord Moynihan, the great British surgeon, had just finished operating before a gallery full of distinguished visiting doctors. He was asked how he could work with such a crowd present. He replied, "You see, there are just three present in the operating room when I operate—the patient and myself." "But that is only two," his questioner commented. "Who is the third?" Moynihan responded, "The third is God."

God—*Religion*

A man met Dr. Billy Graham one day on the street, and after the usual exchange of pleasantries told the spiritual leader of his despair at the sad state of the world. He wound up by saying, "I tell you, Dr. Graham, it's enough to make a man lose his religion." After a moment's reflection, Billy Graham replied, "Rather it seems to me, it's enough to make a man *use* his religion."

Gratitude—*Plagiarism*

I know I don't deserve all the credit for the success. I had help. But then, learning from others is the best formula for success. I recall a story about the great Italian Renaissance artist Raphael. When he was told he had copied one of Michelangelo's pieces, he replied, "A genius takes what he must."

Gratitude—*Woman*

At the end of the 1968 football season, after winning the championship of the American Football League, the players of the victorious New York Jets, with their happy wives, were given a party. Each married player, when called on to speak, glowingly thanked his wife for being a loyal and cooperative helpmate by showing unusual patience and understanding all through the glorious season. When it was the turn of the Jets' fabulous quarterback Broadway Joe Namath to speak, the team's most celebrated playboy-bachelor rose and simply said, "And I want to thank all the good-looking broads in town."

Well, I want to thank all the women for their help—women who, I might say, are wives as well as beautiful broads . . .

Greatness—*Genius*

Once a friend came to the poet Samuel Taylor Coleridge and expressed amazement that he admired "such a small man like William Wordsworth." Coleridge replied, "I don't wonder you think Wordsworth a small man—he runs so far before us all that he dwarfs himself in the distance."

In the same way the man I speak of tonight has been so far ahead of us . . .

Guilt—*Efforts*

We all know in our hearts that we have not done as well as we could have. The late Gil Hodges, while managing the Washington Senators, was informed that four of his players had violated his curfew. Instead of calling them in individually and imposing the customary fine of $100, he addressed the entire squad in the clubhouse. "I know who you are and I don't want to embarrass anybody," he said. "There's a cigar box on my desk. At the end of the day I want to see $400 in it." At the end of the day Hodges found $700 in the box.

History—*Record*

In 1919 Henry Ford was on the witness stand at Mt. Clemens, Michigan. During the course of his libel suit against the Chicago *Tribune* he was reminded by defense counsel that a certain event was a matter of historic record, and the motor magnate exploded: "History is more or less bunk."

Well, despite Henry Ford, I think the public record speaks for itself . . .

⇻

My views are a matter of public record, and I can go along with what Winston Churchill said when he was staying at the White House in December 1941. President Roosevelt was wheeled into Churchill's bedroom and found him emerging naked from his bath. He murmured a word of apology. Churchill brushed it aside and said, "But the Prime Minister of Great Britain has nothing to hide from the President of the United States."

Honor—*Award*

In 1968 the St. Louis Cardinals put up a 10-foot 5-inch bronze statue on a marble pedestal 8 feet high, in front of Busch Stadium, their home ballpark, in honor of Stan Musial, the greatest player in the history of the club. At the dedication, when that statue of Musial was unveiled, the Cards' manager, Red Schoendienst, who had been Musial's teammate and roommate in their playing days, and had remained one of his closest and warmest friends, rose to speak in tribute to the baseball immortal. Looking at the beaming Stan Musial, he said, "In your twenty years as a player for the St. Louis Cardinals you've done a lot for them, and for all baseball. Now you're going to give the pigeons a break."

Hope—*Youth*

When in 1817 John Adams asked his old friend Thomas Jefferson if he would agree to live his seventy-three years over again, Jefferson replied, "Yea, I think, with you, that it is a good world on the whole. My temperament is sanguine. I steer my bark with hope in the head, leaving fear astern."

The writer of the Declaration, in spite of the problems the new country faced, trusted in the youth. And so do I as I reflect . . .

Humanity—*Brotherhood*

In the late nineteenth century a Member of Parliament journeyed to Scotland to make a speech. Alighting from the train in Edinburgh, he took a carriage southward for his destination. But the carriage got mired in mud. To the rescue came a Scottish farmboy who with his team of horses pulled the carriage loose. Afterwards, the politician asked the boy how much they owed him. "Nothing," replied the lad. "Nothing, are you sure?" "Yes." "Is there anything I can do for you. What do you want to do with yourself when you grow up?" "I want to be a doctor." "Well, let me help." True to his word, the aristocratic Englishman helped make it possible for the Scots boy to go to the university.

A little more than a half-century later in another continent, a world statesman lay dangerously ill with pneumonia. Winston Churchill had been stricken while attending a wartime conference in Morocco. But a wonder drug was administered to him— a new drug called penicillin, which had been discovered by Sir Alexander Fleming. Fleming was the young Scottish lad, and the

man who had helped sponsor his education was Randolph Churchill, father of Winston, who recovered through Fleming's miracle
drug.

The bread we cast on waters may come back in the form of
miracles . . .

Humanity—*Magnanimity*

Once Abraham Lincoln was importuned by an old man who was
pleading for a pardon for his son. Lincoln turned to him and gently
but firmly said, "I am sorry, I can do nothing for you. Listen to this
telegram I received from General Butler yesterday: 'President
Lincoln, I pray you not to interfere with the courts-martial of the
army. You will destroy all discipline among our soldiers.'"

Greatly affected by the hopeless despair on the old man's face,
Lincoln said, "By jingo! Butler or no Butler, here goes!" and he
wrote an order and showed it to the old man: "Job Smith is not to
be shot until further orders from me—Abraham Lincoln."

The father expressed disappointment. "Why, I thought it was a
pardon! You may order him to be shot next week."

"My old friend," the President replied, "I see you are not very
well acquainted with me. If your son never dies till orders come
from me to shoot him, he will live to be a great deal older than
Methuselah."

Humility—*Leadership*

When Carlos Romulo, the former President of the Philippines,
won an oratorical contest in the Manila High School as a young
man he ignored the congratulations of one of the other contest-
ants. As he left the auditorium, his father asked, "Why didn't you
shake hands with Julio?" He told his father, "I have no use for Julio,
he was speaking ill of me before the contest." His dignified, gray-
haired father put his arm around his shoulder and said, "Your
grandfather used to tell me that the taller the bamboo grows, the
lower it bends. Remember that always, my boy. The taller the
bamboo grows, the lower it bends."

But we don't have to look all the way to the Philippines for the example of a leader whose hallmark is magnanimity and compassion . . .

Hypocrisy—*Criticism*

The hypocrisy of some of my critics amazes me. I can understand the way Senator Millard Tydings of Maryland felt when some of the more bibulous Senators attacked him for supporting the repeal of Prohibition. Tydings replied, "To paraphrase the words of the apostle Matthew, 'Let he who is without gin, cast the first vote.' "

Idea—*Imagination*

Once Thomas Edison was praised at a dinner as a "unique genius." Edison said, "No! Actually, I am a good sponge. I absorb ideas and put them to use. Most of my ideas first belonged to people who did not bother to develop them."

Ideals—*Crisis*

During the darkest days of the Civil War, Abraham Lincoln had the burden of sustaining the hopes and goals of the Union cause. Once when a delegation called at the White House and detailed a catalogue of crises facing America, Lincoln told this story: "Years ago a young friend and I were out one night when a shower of meteors fell from the clear November sky. The young man was frightened, but I told him to look up in the sky past the shooting stars to the fixed stars beyond, shining serene in the firmament, and I said, 'Let us not mind the meteors, but let us keep our eyes on the stars.' "

What Lincoln was saying, in effect, is that a country or a political party must stay true to its ideals . . .

Ideas—*Proposals*

A Concord farmer who was a friend of Ralph Waldo Emerson saw a book of Plato in his library and asked to borrow it. A month later when he returned, Emerson asked how he enjoyed it. "I liked it," replied his neighbor. "This Plato has a lot of my ideas."

The test of any brilliant man is when the people begin to adopt and quote his ideas . . .

Ignorance—*Education*

Shortly before his death Chief Justice Melville W. Fuller presided at a church conference. During a heated debate, a delegate rose and began a tirade against universities and education, giving thanks to God that he had never been corrupted by any contact with a college. "Do I understand the speaker thanks God for his ignorance?" interrupted Chief Justice Fuller. "Well, yes, if you want to put it that way" was the answer. "All I have to say then," said the Chief Justice, "is that you have a great deal to be thankful for."

Well, today we have a lot to be thankful for in the way of educational opportunities . . .

Image—*Facade*

George Allen, adviser and close friend of three Presidents— Franklin Roosevelt, Truman, and Eisenhower, claimed his start as political insider began during World War II. In the early part of the war, he was traveling to London. Americans in key roles over there waylaid him to catch the latest gossip. "Who's going to come over in the Allied Command?" one asked. Allen reflected and then whispered something he recently overheard from a couple of generals in a golf game: "Watch a guy from Kansas named Eisenhower." Sure enough, a month later Eisenhower was appointed head of SHAEF. Allen was thought to be wired to the top. But the fact remained—Allen had never met Eisenhower. When he was returning to London some months later, he realized his credibility would be shattered when people realized that Ike didn't even know his name. So he bit the bullet and called SHAEF headquarters and asked to speak to the general on a private matter. "General," he said, "I'm George Allen—you don't know me and that's a source of considerable embarrassment. You see, everyone here thinks that we're friends. Could I come over and see you so that you will recognize me when you run into me?" Ike laughed at the candor of the suggestion. "Better than that," said Ike, "I'll be at the Savoy Hotel dining room at one P.M. for lunch. You come in at five past and say in a loud voice, 'Hello, Ike' and I'll say, 'Good to see you again, George.'" They did just that. In fact, Ike asked Allen to just keep whispering his funny stories into his ear. The result was that word got back that Allen was a key adviser to Eisenhower and his reputation was made.

Imitation—*Potential*

Some years ago a dinner was held in Hollywood to celebrate Charlie Chaplin's birthday. Chaplin entertained the guests throughout the evening by imitating people with whom they were familiar: friends, his chauffeur, his servants, his secretaries. Finally he sang at the top of his voice an aria from an Italian opera and sang it superbly. "Why, Charlie, I never knew you could sing so beautifully," a guest exclaimed. "I can't sing at all," Chaplin rejoined. "I was only imitating Caruso."

When we emulate the best, we bring out the best in ourselves . . .

Immodesty—*Truth*

In the 1940s Notre Dame's star center, Frankie Szymanski, appeared in a South Bend court as a witness in a civil suit. "Are you on the Notre Dame football team this year?" queried the judge. "Yes," replied Szymanski. "Are you their star quarterback?" asked the judge. "Yes," answered Frankie, "I hear one sportswriter considers me the finest all-round athlete South Bend, Indiana, has seen in many a year."

After the trial Notre Dame Coach Frank Leahy came up to Szymanski and said, "Frankie, you certainly weren't too modest up on the stand." "I guess not, Coach," replied Szymanski. "But gee whiz—what would I say?—after all I was under oath."

Well, if I were put under oath, I'd have to say our company is the finest in the field . . .

Impossibility—*Challenge*

Once Napoleon suddenly appeared at one of his camps at Bou-logne-sur-Mer. His first words to Marshal Soult on arrival were, "How much time do you require to be able to embark?" "Three days, sire." "I can only give you one," replied Napoleon. "That's impossible," said the Marshal. " 'Impossible' is not a word in my dictionary. Erase it from yours," commanded Napoleon.

Inaction—*Delay*

We hear much about the extent of progress but so far the indications of any real results approximate the work playwright Marc Connelly once claimed to have done. The author of *The Green Pastures* was being hounded by a producer to whom he had promised a new play. "Marc," he demanded, "where's that play? I want to get the cast assembled."

"It's coming along," Connelly assured him vaguely. "Just how much have you actually done?" asked the producer. "Well," said Connelly, "you know it's to be in three acts and two intermissions. I've just finished the intermissions."

And that's about all the work . . .

Incentive—*Ambition*

Simon Cameron, the Secretary of War under Lincoln, was once asked why his son, who was smart, attractive, and had all the advantages of his father's influence and prestige behind him, had not done so well in politics.

"Donald is a likely fellow and will do well," Simon Cameron replied, "but you must remember that I started life with a big advantage over him." "What was that?" was the question. "Poverty," replied Cameron.

Incentive is the spur to any career. The problem with bureaucracy or tenure in education jobs is that security stifles drive . . .

Incredibility—*Naïveté*

The naïveté we have just heard expressed reminds me of the time the celebrated Duke of Wellington was walking down Piccadilly in London. Upon being approached by a stranger who greeted him with "Mr. Smith, I believe," the Duke responded, "If you believe that, sir, you will believe anything."

Ineffectual—*Blessing*

I will, of course, give it my blessing but I am not convinced it will do much good. It reminds me of an incident during the Civil War. A man who wanted to get to Confederate Richmond asked President Lincoln for a presidential pass. It was at that time when Lincoln was so exasperated by General McClellan's reluctance to attack Lee and his forces in Virginia. "I would be very happy to oblige you if my passes were respected; but the fact is, sir, I have within the last two years given passes to 250,000 men to go to Richmond and not one has got there yet."

Injury—*Health*

Back in the 1930s one of the hitters' favorite pitchers was a hurler for the Brooklyn Dodgers, "Boom-Boom" Beck. "Boom-Boom" was called that because batters slammed his offerings like shots into the outfield. One afternoon, enemy bats were shelling "Boom-Boom" Beck heavier than usual. He stormed into his dugout and violently kicked the water bucket. "Here, here, cut that out!" manager Casey Stengel gently warned him. "If you break your leg, I can't trade you!"

In the same sense we don't want anything to happen to one of our favorite . . .

In-Laws—*Family*

Shortly after World War II, an American colonel and his wife, stationed in London, happened to meet with Sarah Churchill and her then husband Vic Oliver, a music hall comedian of the Milton Berle variety. Oliver had the unfortunate habit of calling his father-in-law, Winston Churchill, "Popsy," which understandably did little to endear him to the old statesman. At any rate, Vic and Sarah invited the American couple down to Chartwell one Sunday evening after the two Americans had professed their great admiration for the wartime prime minister.

The Sunday evening at Chartwell started with Churchill glowering and saying very little. But Oliver, who wanted his American friends to see something of the great man in action, tried to spark conversation with this question: "Popsy, who do you think was the greatest statesman you ever knew?" Churchill, without even looking up, said, "Without a doubt, the greatest statesman I ever knew was Benito Mussolini." After some silence by a flabbergasted audience, Oliver made this follow-up query: "But, Popsy, why do you pick Mussolini?" "Because," growled Churchill, "Mussolini is the only statesman who had the requisite courage to have his son-in-law executed" (Count Ciano, Italian Foreign Secretary, in 1943).

Well, I am happy to say that the only shooting I have done of my in-laws has been with a camera . . .

Inspiration—*Excellence*

Before Lou Little became the most successful football coach in Columbia University history, he occupied a similar post at Georgetown University. One year, there was a youngster on the squad who was no great shakes as a football player, but whose personality served as a morale booster for the whole team. Little was deeply fond of the boy. He liked the proud way he walked arm-in-arm with his father on the campus from time to time. If the team was far enough ahead, Little even let him get into a game occasionally for the last few minutes of play.

One day, about a week before the big finale with Fordham, the boy's mother called Little on the phone. "My husband died this morning of a heart attack," she said. "Will you break the news to my boy? He'll take it better if it comes from you." Little did what was necessary, and the boy went home sorrowfully. He was back three days later, and came straight to Lou Little. "Coach," he begged, "I want to ask something of you that means an awful lot to me. I want to start in that game against Fordham. I think it's what my father would have liked most." Little hesitated, and then agreed. "Okay, son, you'll start, but you'll only be in there for a play or two. You aren't quite good enough, and you know it."

True to his word, Little started the boy—but never took him out. For sixty full, jarring minutes he played inspired football—running, blocking, and tackling like an All-American, and sparking the team to victory. Back in the clubhouse, Little threw his arm around the boy's shoulder and said, "Son, you were terrific today. You stayed in because you belonged there. You never played that kind of football before. What got into you?"

The boy answered, "Remember how my father and I used to go about arm-in-arm? There was something about him very few people knew. Dad was blind. And I knew today would be the first time he would ever see me play."

And there are those who have gone before us who will be watching how we play—and we are going to give more than we thought we were capable of . . .

Inspiration—*Genius*

Jacques Lipchitz, the sculptor, spent his youth in Paris, where he was a close friend of Soutine, Modigliani, and Chagall. One day a friend complained that he was dissatisfied with the light he painted on his canvases, and went off to Morocco, seeking a change in light. He found, however, that the light in his Moroccan canvases was no different. Lipchitz then advised him, "An artist's light comes from within, not from without."

Instincts—*Ideas*

Once Josephus Daniels, Secretary of the Navy under Woodrow Wilson, related how he had asked Andrew Carnegie what was the secret of his remarkable success. Carnegie replied, "I owe it all to my flashes." Mystified, Daniels said, "What do you mean by 'flashes'?" "All my life," replied Carnegie, "I woke up early in the morning, and always there came into my mind with the waking a flash telling me what to do that day, and if I followed those matin flashes, I always succeeded." "You mean," said Daniels, "that you have heavenly visions, and like the man in the scriptures you were not disobedient to your visions?" "Call it that if you like," answered Carnegie, "or call it flashes; but it was the following of those silent admonitions and directions which brought me the success you say I have achieved."

Well, some would call those silent admonitions Carnegie was talking about "a feeling in my heart," "gut knowledge," a "strong hunch." And my instincts about this proposal . . .

Institution—*Enduring*

As we think back to the beginning of this movement, I am reminded of what the noted seventeenth-century woman of French letters Madame de Sévigné once predicted to her circle at the Hôtel de Rambouillet: "Racine will go out of fashion like coffee."

Well, like Racine and coffee, this movement has not failed . . .

Integrity—*Honesty*

At the close of the Civil War, Robert E. Lee was offered the presidency of a large insurance firm. Lee replied that he did not feel his services would be worth the $50,000 salary offered. "We aren't interested in your services," the man replied. "We merely want your name." "That," said General Lee quietly, "is not for sale."

Introduction—*Fame*

In all the history of public relations, no one craved free publicity more than P. T. Barnum. When he was near death, an editor of the *Evening Sun*, in New York, asked the great showman's publicity agent if Barnum would like having his obituary published before he died. The agent said, "The old man will be delighted." The next day Barnum read four columns about his own death, and he loved it.

Well, that introduction seemed better suited for a eulogy. Anyway, I'm glad I didn't have to die to hear it . . .

Introduction—*Qualifications*

When I think of some of the distinguished people at the head table whose names, lineage, and accomplishments are so famous, I think of Abraham Lincoln, when running for the Illinois state legislature. He had an opponent of considerable standing and in one debate this adversary dwelt on the fact that his father had been Senator, his grandfather a general, and his uncle a Congressman. Abe then rose to give his family background with this comment: "Ladies and Gentlemen, I come from a long line of married folks."

Introduction—*Unfamiliar*

It is my responsibility to introduce our speaker—one whom I know well, but all of you do not. That, I assure you, is a misfortune which soon will be rectified. In that sense it is unlike a situation in which Abraham Lincoln once found himself while arguing a case. The opposing counsel objected to a juror on the ground that he knew Mr. Lincoln, and since to deny the objection would have reflected upon the honor of the lawyer, the judge allowed the juror to be disqualified. But when Lincoln, following the example of his adversary, examined two or three of the proposed jury and found that they knew his opponent, the judge interfered. "Now, Mr. Lincoln," he observed severely, "you are wasting time. The mere fact that a juror knows your opponent does not disqualify him." "No, Your Honor," responded Lincoln dryly, "but I am afraid some of the gentlemen may not know him, which would place me at a disadvantage."

Well, I assure that is not the case here . . .

Investment—*Advertisement*

John Wanamaker, the first great department store entrepreneur, began business in 1861 with his brother-in-law on a capital investment of $3,500. They could not afford a horse and wagon so John Wanamaker purchased a two-wheeled cart and delivered the first order himself. The profits of that first day's business were $36, and

Wanamaker used it to buy an advertisement in the Philadelphia *Inquirer* the next day.

Investment—*Cheap*

As the saying goes, you get out of something what you put into it. Once William Hogarth, the eminent English painter, was commissioned by a cheap millionaire to portray on canvas an incident from the Old Testament. Hogarth named his price, and the millionaire proceeded to beat him down to about one-third of that sum. Hogarth finally agreed to do the painting at this absurdly low figure. When, some time later, Hogarth invited him in to view the painting, he was surprised to find only a huge blot of red paint on the canvas. "What is it?" he asked. "The crossing of the Red Sea by the children of Israel, and their pursuit by the Egyptians," replied Hogarth. As he pointed to the blotch of red paint, he added, "This is the Red Sea." "Oh, and where are the Egyptians?" asked the miser. "They were all drowned," responded Hogarth. "And the Israelites?" "They have all crossed over!"

Well, the message is, you can't expect to get something for nothing . . .

Invocation—*Conference*

In the 1787 Constitutional Convention when the big states were deadlocked against the small states, wise old Benjamin Franklin rose to offer a motion: "I have lived, sir, a long time; and the longer I live the more convincing proofs I see of this truth that God governs in the affairs of men. And if a sparrow cannot fall to the ground without His notice, is it probable that an empire can rise without His aid? We have been assured, sir, in the sacred writings, that 'Except the Lord build the house, they labor in vain that build it.' I firmly believe this; I also believe that, without His concurring aid, we shall succeed in this political building no better than the builders of Babel; I therefore beg leave to move that henceforth prayers, imploring the assistance of heaven and its blessing on our deliberations, be held in this assembly every morning before we proceed to business; and that one or more of the clergy of this city be requested to officiate in that service."

In the tradition of Franklin and our Founding Fathers, let us begin our deliberations with prayer . . .

Involvement—*Injustice*

Ralph Waldo Emerson once called at the Concord jail to see his friend Henry David Thoreau. Thoreau had been sentenced for refusing to pay taxes to a town that supported drilling for the Mexican War, a war which he deemed a move to extend slavery. The exponent of Self-Reliance was puzzled by the situation. "Henry," he said, "why are you here?" "Waldo," asked Thoreau, "why are you not here?"

Involvement—*Participation*

It is easy to be a social critic. But unless you are involved, you are part of the problem not part of the solution. Zebulon Vance when he was Governor of North Carolina in the late nineteenth century once met a venerable Negro Baptist minister when he was driving his buggy to church. He stopped his horse and called to the old man: "Reverend, I suppose you are walking down the road to Shiloh Baptist Church?"

"Yes, Governor, I am going to Shiloh to preach this morning."

"Well, Reverend, Shiloh is still a mile away. Can I give you a lift?"

When the journey was resumed, the governor said to the old preacher, "Well, Reverend, you are a Baptist."

"Yes, Governor, I am a Baptist."

"Well, Reverend, you know I am a Presbyterian."

"Yes, Governor. Everybody in North Carolina knows you are a Presbyterian."

"Well, Reverend, there is one thing I'd like to know. Do you preach to your people the doctrine of election?"

"Yes, Governor, I preach the doctrine of election. But I preach it a little different from what you Presbyterians preach it."

"How different, Reverend?"

"Well, Governor, I preach to my people the doctrine of election all right, but I'm always careful to tell my people that they ain't nobody going to be elected what ain't a candidate."

Irrationality—*Significance*

Back in 1960 when Soviet Premier Nikita Khrushchev came to the United Nations, he created quite a stir in the Assembly when, in a heated tirade, he took off his shoe and pounded on the table with it. In the best tradition of British unflappability, Prime Minister Harold Macmillan remarked calmly, "I'd like that translated, if I may."

Similarly, I like to find out the meaning of the latest irrational behavior . . .

Judiciary—*Legal System*

When Thaddeus Stevens was a young lawyer, he once had a case before a bad-tempered judge of an obscure Pennsylvania court. Under what he considered a very erroneous ruling, the case was decided against him. Stevens threw down his books and picked up his hat in a state of indignation, scattering imprecations all around him. The judge assumed an air of offended majesty, and asked Stevens if he meant to "express your contempt for this court." Stevens turned to him very politely, made a respectful bow, and feigned amazement. "Express my contempt for this court? No, sir. I am trying to conceal it, Your Honor, but I find it damned hard to do."

And today many are finding it difficult to conceal their contempt for a legal system that condones a revolving-door release for hardened criminals . . .

Justice—*Exploited*

When Sir Thomas More was lord chancellor in the reign of Henry VIII, he ordered a gentleman to pay a sum of money to a poor woman whom he had wronged. The gentleman said, "Then I hope your lordship will grant me a long day to pay it." "I will grant your motion," said the chancellor. "Monday next is St. Barnabas's day, which is the longest day in the year. Pay it to the widow on that day, or I will commit you to the Fleet prison."

It is time for us to begin redressing the grievances of some of our most exploited . . .

Kindness—*Introduction*

Our speaker is someone we all know and love. His very face bespeaks his innate warmth and generosity. And I don't think that's purely genetics either. I recall once that one of Abraham Lincoln's advisers urgently recommended a certain man for a post in the cabinet. When Lincoln declined to follow the suggestion, he was asked to give his reasons. "I don't like the man's face," the President explained. "But the poor man isn't responsible for his face," his advocate insisted. "Every man over forty is responsible for his face," Lincoln replied.

Law—*Defeat*

When Senator Sam Ervin of North Carolina was a circuit judge in his state, he had to decide a case which had been argued by two lawyers. After he had rendered his decision and retired to chambers, the sheriff came in. "Your Honor," he said, "Jim Spofford's out there on the street cussin' you a-fierce. He's got a crowd around him, givin' you the dickens. Do you want to cite him for contempt? Shall I bring him in?" "He's the one I decided against?" asked Ervin. "Yes, sir." "Well, just ignore it. It's the privilege of a lawyer to cuss the court for a reasonable length of time after he loses a case."

So looking at it that way, I am not too concerned about the criticism from that particular quarter . . .

Law—*Justice*

Around 1930 two great jurists found themselves in conversation at a dinner. Learned Hand, the distinguished New York appellate judge, argued a point of law with Justice Oliver Wendell Holmes. "But," said Judge Hand, "we're talking about a court of justice." "No," said Justice Holmes, "it is only a court of law."

Holmes meant that justice is an infinite ideal like truth, but the courts are only instruments of man . . .

Law—*Overwhelmed*

Chief Justice John Marshall was very fond of doing everything himself and objected strongly to any assistance being rendered him. One day when he was an old man, wishing to consult some work of reference, he entered the law library and proceeded to mount a set of steps and draw out a book from an upper shelf. The books, being tightly packed together, refused to leave one without the others, and the chief justice, not noticing this, in withdrawing the one he wished, dislodged the entire row, which came down, felling him to the floor. The librarian instantly ran to the rescue, inquiring whether the venerable jurist was hurt and offering his assistance. "Let me alone," said Marshall. "I am a little stunned for the moment. That is all. I have laid down the law often, but this is the first time the law has ever laid me down."

Well, in another sense we are becoming overwhelmed by the proliferation of laws, statutes, and decisions—federal and state, administrative and legislative . . .

Law—*Purpose*

Justice Joseph Story once explained the difference between himself and Chief Justice John Marshall. "Marshall would say to me here is the law—now you must find the authorities. You see, when I examine a case I go from headland to headland searching out each case. But Marshall has a compass in his head. He knows exactly where he is going and goes exactly to his result."

Lawyer—*Profession*

The English barrister Sir John Maynard once put down the infamous Judge George Jeffreys. The old "hanging judge" told Maynard in a trial, "Sir, you have grown so old you have forgotten the law." Sir John replied, "I have forgotten more law than you ever knew, but allow me to say, I have not forgotten much."

Layout—*Accommodations*

Just a word to our hosts to thank them for the fabulous accommo-
dations and arrangements. It makes me think of what Alexander
Woollcott once said about playwright Moss Hart's spread in Bucks
County. He had bought a big estate in Pennsylvania that was
landscaped within an inch of its life—rows of privet hedges and
circles of dwarf pines everywhere. Woollcott went to visit him one
day, and as he stepped out of the car, Hart asked him what he
thought of the place. "Well," said Woollcott, "it only shows what
God could do if he had enough money."

Leader—*Respect*

In the seventeenth century an English ambassador to France,
Lord Herbert, paid honor to a distinguished French soldier—that
brave general the Duke of Lesdiguières, who was now grown very
old and deaf. The Frenchman's first words were, "Monsieur, you
must do me the honor to speak loud, for I am deaf." Herbert
answered him, "You were born to command and not to obey, it
is enough if others have ears to hear you."

Well, if there was one born to command, it is our speaker tonight . . .

Leadership—*Executive*

When the venerable Benjamin Franklin was ambassador to the
French court, he won many hearts by his ready turn of phrase. At
a diplomatic dinner in 1781, all the big nations were present,
including Britain, and Franklin was representing the newly independent United States of America.

The French foreign secretary opened the dinner by toasting his
king in champagne: "To His Majesty, King Louis, the Sun, whose
shining presence radiates the earth of France."

The British ambassador then rose to give his toast: "To King
George the Third, the Moon, whose brilliance lights up the skies
of Britain."

Then the aging Franklin rose and said with a twinkle: "I cannot give you the sun nor the moon, but I give you General George Washington of the United States, the Joshua who made the Sun and the Moon stand still when he commanded."

Today I would like to toast another man who with his executive skills made his competition look as if they were standing still . . .

Leadership—*Magnanimity*

Alexander the Great, sitting in judgment on one of his subjects, found him guilty and sentenced him to death. "I appeal," said the man. "Appeal? To whom?" asked Alexander. "I am the highest authority." "Your Majesty," said the condemned man, "I appeal from Alexander the Small to Alexander the Great."

All of us have, as Lincoln said, an angel side of our natures . . .

Leadership—*Responsiveness*

In 1860 a little spindly-legged nine-year-old named Grace Bedell, who lived in the upstate New York village of Westfield, saw a picture of the newly elected President of the United States. She thought he would be better looking and more impressive if he grew whiskers, and what is more, she sat down and wrote him so. Mr. Lincoln, amused, gravely replied that people might accuse him of silly affectation for sprouting a beard at this stage of his career. No, answered Grace, it was the right thing for him to do, for he looked too solemn, and she believed other little girls, like herself, would be scared of him without whiskers.

When Mr. Lincoln's special train carried him from Illinois to New York, and then on to his inauguration in Washington, he ordered a stop at Westfield, and from the rear platform announced, "I have a correspondent in this town named Grace Bedell, and if she's present, I hope she'll step forward." "Here I am," called the astonished Grace. "Well, Grace," beamed Mr. Lincoln, leaning over the rear rail, "you see, I let these whiskers grow for you! I hope you think I'm better looking now!" "You look wonderful now," she assured him, "and I bet you're going to be the greatest President this country ever had!" Mr. Lincoln put his stovepipe hat back on his head, the train puffed away—and maybe one or two spectators realized that they had just seen an example of American democracy really clicking on every cylinder.

Presidents and politicians must never isolate themselves . . .

Leadership—*Stewardship*

On one occasion when General Andrew Jackson was sailing down the Chesapeake Bay in an old steamboat with the waves running high, an elderly gentleman expressed some concern. "You are uneasy," said Old Hickory to him. "I see you never sailed before with me."

We have sailed through some difficult times with our leader, but I assure you we have never been uneasy . . .

Leadership—*Successful*

In the Civil War there were continual rumors of General Grant's fondness for the bottle. As Lincoln's one winning commander, Grant was too good to lose, even though demands streamed in weekly asking for Grant's removal. One day a delegation headed by a distinguished doctor of divinity from New York called on him and made the familiar complaint against Grant. After the clergyman had concluded his remarks, Lincoln asked if any others desired to add anything to what had already been said. They replied that they did not. Then looking as serious as he could, he said, "Doctor, can you tell me where General Grant gets his liquor?" The reverend doctor seemed quite nonplussed and replied that he could not. Lincoln then said to him, "I am very sorry, for if you could tell me, I would direct the chief quartermaster of the army to lay in a large stock of the same kind of liquor and would also direct him to furnish a supply to some of my other generals who have never yet won a victory."

I have heard many comments about the life-style of the next speaker. To put it clearly, he does appreciate the finer things of life, but in that same spirit nothing he puts his hand to lacks the touch of excellence . . .

Legacy—*Accumulation*

In 1791 Benjamin Franklin left a fund of $5,000 to the City of Boston. His will provided that interest from this fund be allowed to accumulate for a hundred years. By 1891 the $5,000 had grown to almost $400,000. A school was established with part of the accumulated fund and the balance, $92,000, was invested for a second century. It was reported that by 1950 the $92,000 had increased to almost a million. Apparently Ben knew what he was talking about when he said, "Money begets money and its offspring begets more."

Legislature—*Speech*

One day when Winston Churchill was crossing the House of Commons yard, he was greeted by a young member. Churchill returned the greeting and said, "Aren't you making your maiden speech today?" The young Parliamentarian said yes and told of his great apprehensions. "Good," said Churchill. "You ought to have a little fear and humility before making your first speech. But let me give you some words of advice. Just before I start speaking, I always look around me and reflect: what a lot of damn fools—then I feel a lot better."

Now after my first term in the legislature, I have come to see the wisdom of Churchill's remarks. Not only am I not so shy but also am more aware after reading some of the proposed bills of what a lot of damn fools some of them are . . .

Liberalism—*Humanity*

Once Aristotle was being censured for giving charity to a man whose character was without merit. He replied, "I did not give it to the man, I gave it to humanity."

And in the same sense we owe it to humanity to better conditions in prisons even for the most hardened criminals . . .

Life—*Age*

Once you lose your curiosity about life, your sense of exploration, you have lost the gift of living. Shortly before John Dewey's ninetieth birthday, he was interviewed by a reporter.

"What is the good of all your thinking?" the reporter asked. "Where does it get you?"

Dewey replied quietly, "The good is that which lies in climbing mountains."

"Climbing mountains?" questioned the young man. "What is the good of doing that?"

"You see other mountains," was the reply. "When you are no longer interested in climbing mountains to see other mountains to climb, then life is over."

And when you are no longer open to new interests, or curious about what new things are developing, your life is over . . .

Life—*Enjoyment*

When Geraldine Farrar, the former opera star, was interviewed on her eightieth birthday, she was asked her secret of longevity. She answered, "Taking time to taste life. So much is pressing on humans today that no one has time to stand still long enough to evaluate it. They gulp life and taste nothing! They eat life and have no savor."

Well, here is one who has tasted life to the fullest . . .

Life—*Excellence*

On Arturo Toscanini's eightieth birthday, someone asked his son, Walter, what his father ranked as his most important achievement. The son replied, "For him there can be no such thing. Whatever he happens to be doing at the moment is the biggest thing in his life, whether it is conducting a symphony or peeling an orange."

And in what our speaker has been doing for the last few months, he has given it the attention worthy of the most important thing in his life . . .

Listener—*Responsiveness*

When Calvin Coolidge was Vice President, his successor as Governor of Massachusetts, Channing Cox, paid him a visit. Cox asked how Coolidge had been able to see so many visitors a day when he was governor, yet always leave the office at 5 P.M., while Cox himself found he often left as late as 9 P.M. "Why the difference?" he asked. Coolidge replied, "You talk back."

And more of our politicians should do less talking and more listening . . .

Logic—*Fallacious*

When the hard-drinking Hack Wilson was slugging for the Brooklyn Dodgers, his abstemious manager Max Carey called a meeting of the entire team. Although Wilson was hitting .300 for the Dodgers and pumping out homers he had to be saved somehow! So Carey tried the psychological approach: health, doctors' warnings, and all that. As he called the player meeting to order, Max stood at a table on which he had placed two glasses and a plate of live angleworms. One glass was filled with water, the other with gin, Wilson's favorite elixir. With a flourish, the manager dropped a worm in the glass of water. It wriggled happily. Now Max plunged the same worm into the gin; it stiffened and expired. A murmur ran through the room and some of the players were obviously impressed. Not Wilson. Hack didn't even seem interested. Carey waited a little, hoping for some delayed reaction from his wayward member. When none came, he prodded, "That mean anything to you, Wilson?" "Sure, Skipper," answered Hack. "It proves if you drink gin you'll never have no worms!"

The same kind of logic characterizes the arguments of our friends. They say . . .

Losses—*War*

Shortly after the last war a general was talking to Albert Einstein at Princeton. "Our losses in the last military campaign were relatively mild," the army officer commented with deep pride. "Relative to what?" asked the inventor of the theory.

Magnanimity—*Forgiveness*

Clara Barton, the founder of the nursing profession, never was known to hold resentment against anyone. One time a friend recalled to her a cruel thing that had happened to her some years previously, but Clara seemed not to remember the incident. "Don't you remember the wrong that was done to you?" the friend asked Clara. "No," Clara answered calmly, "I distinctly remember forgetting that."

It takes a magnanimous person who is too big to remember little slights . . .

Market—*Boldness*

Sometimes it takes daring and imagination to sense the potential of a great market. In December 1936 an American business executive walked briskly down the airplane ramp and set foot in France for the first time. The customs official looked in his suitcase and found samples of cosmetics. "You are bringing cosmetics from America to sell to France?" the official asked skeptically. "Yes," the passenger said, "my name is Factor." "Well, you don't have a chance." "You may be right," said Davis Factor, son of Max Factor, "but my father is convinced we have something women want."

And, like Factor, I have faith that the American people want . . .

Market—*Consumer*

An idea born more than fifty years ago was to revolutionize the retail business. A Memphis businessman named Clarence Saunders, founder of the Piggly Wiggly food store chain, had this idea: "If only," he would tell friends, "you would let the customer get close to the merchandise so that he could pick it up and examine it carefully, he would buy it. Give impulse buying a chance."

Similarly, our task today is to get the potential buyer next to our product . . .

Market—*Need*

It was 1893, a year of financial panic. A young graduate from Washington University in St. Louis named William Danforth asked his father whether it was the right time to go into business. His father told him that economically poor times are times of opportunity. "Son," the father said, "get into a business that fills a need for lots of people—something they need all year around in good times and bad." The son took the advice and formed what became the Ralston Purina company.

Similarly, I sense a growing market today . . .

Market—*Product*

I think it is time to examine our product. We cannot assume the viewpoint of Oscar Wilde. The British playwright arrived at his club one evening after witnessing a first production of a play of his that was a complete failure. "Oscar, how did your play go to-night?" asked a friend. "Oh," was the lofty response, "the play was a great success but the audience was a failure."

Marriage—*Alliance*

At the time when Leland Hayward was one of the most successful talent agents in Hollywood, he married his beautiful and talented client Margaret Sullavan. One of his waggish friends sent him a telegram saying, "Congratulations on getting the other 90 percent."

Well, in this merger we are getting 100 percent at least in terms of . . .

Marriage—*Bachelor*

In Athens Socrates was approached by one of his students. The young man asked: "Do you think a man should marry or remain single?" "Whichever you do, you will repent of it, my friend," replied the philosopher.

Well, I think our friend here with his beautiful wife would make Socrates repent of his advice . . .

Martyr—*Survival*

Former Secretary of State William Seward and Thurlow Weed, political boss of New York, were riding up Broadway one day and passed the bronze statue of Lincoln in Union Square. Seward, who once was almost nominated President, told Weed, "If you had stayed loyal to me, I would have had a bronze statue there instead of Lincoln." "Seward," replied Weed, "is it not better to be alive with me than dead in bronze?"

And, similarly, I'm just as glad that I ducked the chance to run against the Senator . . .

Materialism—*Values*

Money cannot be the only consideration. The naturalist Louis Agassiz Fuertes understood this. Once he had declined to deliver a lecture before some lyceum or public society on account of the inroads which previous lectures given by him had made upon his studies and thought. The gentleman who had been assigned to invite him continued to press the invitation, assuring him that the society was ready to pay him liberally for his services. "That is no inducement to me," replied Fuertes. "I cannot afford to waste my time in making money."

Mediocre—*Half-hearted*

You can't succeed unless you go all out. Your heart and soul have to be completely involved. You can't run the bases, for example, the way Tony Cuccinello once did for Casey Stengel. Cuccinello laid into a fat pitch one day and sent it on a line against the center-field concrete. Brooklyn Manager Stengel, who was coaching at third, saw a fine rally in the making and signaled frantically to Tony to come on. The batter rounded first in high gear, touched second, and lit out for third. Casey put down his hands indicating that Tony should slide into the bag. The runner would have made it by a comfortable margin had he obeyed instructions, but he came into the bag relaxed and standing, and the third baseman slapped the ball on him to bring the promising rally to an abrupt close. Casey let out an agonized screech and grabbed Cuccinello by the throat. "You big bum!" Casey screamed. "What's the idea of coming in like that? Why didn't you slide like I told you?" A wounded look crossed Tony's honest face. "Oh, I couldn't Casey," he protested, "I would have busted all the cigars in my pocket."

Well, if we are really serious, it means we are going to have to give up a few things . . .

Mediocre—*Inadequate*

My reaction to the whole performance reminds me of a short column Dorothy Parker did for *Vanity Fair*. She was reviewing Channing Pollock's *House Beautiful* and she capsulized it in one sentence: "The *House Beautiful* is the play lousy."

Mediocre—*Ineffectual*

I won't comment on the Senator's speech. My reaction is much like that of writer George Kaufman. When he was asked what he thought of a play opening. "It's not quite fair for me to say," Kaufman commented. "I saw it under peculiarly unfortunate circumstances. The curtain was up."

And similarly I watched the Senator's televised speech with the audio on . . .

Mediocrity—*Mess*

Oswald Jacoby, the noted bridge expert, was being harassed by many questions from his neophyte bridge partner. After she had butchered a hand that was an easy game, she asked, "And do tell me, Mr. Jacoby, how would you have played the hand under the same circumstances?" "Madam," said Mr. Jacoby tersely, "I would have played it under an assumed name."

And I wouldn't think anyone would want to take the credit for the mess . . .

Mediocrity—*Office*

The curious chain of events that landed this man in office reminds me of what Lord Edward Thurlow once said in the House of Lords about Augustus Henry Grafton, 3rd Duke of Grafton. In reply to a speech by Grafton he said, "Does he not feel that he owes his seat in this chamber as being the accident of an accident?"

Mediocrity—*Position*

The talents and qualifications of the gentleman are overwhelming. It reminds me of the famous letter President Truman wrote to music critic Paul Hume, who had described Margaret Truman's singing at Constitution Hall a couple of days before as "flat." Truman said, "You sound like an eight-ulcer man on a four-ulcer job."

Memorial—*Observance*

In March 1977 President Carter dispatched the Woodcock Mission to Hanoi to find out what happened to those servicemen still listed as Missing in Action. Besides Leonard Woodcock the delegation included former Senator Mike Mansfield and Congressman G. V. ("Sonny") Montgomery, a Democrat from Mississippi. One morning the group was led to a cement floor basement. There two Viet Cong officials had hauled out the crated remains of eight Americans.

As the transfer was being made, Sonny Montgomery was moved by the occasion. "I believe," he said in a broken voice, "I believe this calls for some ceremony." Montgomery then withdrew to a small dark room off the warehouse platform and with the boxes in front of him offered a silent prayer.

Similarly, I think some observance is in order now—perhaps some moments of silence for those of our own ancestors and forefathers whose names are unknown outside their own immediate families and whose sacrifices are little appreciated . . .

Memorial—*Plaque*

In 1964 former President Truman visited Athens. His hosts, dignitaries of the Greek government, offered to show him the statue of him erected to memorialize Greek gratitude for his Truman Doctrine, an aid plan that helped thwart Communist takeover. Truman rejected the offer, saying, "There should be no memorial to a living man."

Because of similar qualms I hesitate to speak about my own efforts in the past. I would like to talk about all of our hopes for the future . . .

Memory—*Expert*

When Arturo Toscanini was a young man, he played the cello. He was extremely nearsighted, and in order to avoid bending close to the music, he memorized his part as well as the parts for every instrument in the orchestra. One night, the conductor of the La Scala orchestra took ill. Fellow musicians suggested that Toscanini do the conducting. The audience was amused at the poise of the nineteen-year-old boy and was very interested to see what he could do. He closed the score book and conducted the entire program from memory, receiving a tumultuous ovation.

In a similar way, our speaker knows his subject by heart . . .

Mess—*Problem*

Just after the first world war a debate occurred in the Massachusetts state legislature in which passions were hotly aroused. In fact, one senator used the unparliamentary expression "Go to hell." The object of the abusive curse called on the then Governor Calvin Coolidge to see if there were some rules calling for a reprimand. Coolidge replied, "Senator, I've looked up the law and you don't have to go there."

And we don't have to go blindly down the path to perdition that we have been following either . . .

Mind—*Investment*

Young Benjamin Disraeli once went to see Henry Podwick to borrow money. The wealthy backer of Conservative Party causes asked his visitor, "What security do you have to offer for these few thousand pounds you ask me to lend you?" "My brains," was the reply. "I accept the security," said the financier, who later was elated with Disraeli's successes.

And in another sense we can say we have benefitted from the mind and ideas of our speaker . . .

Mistake—*Intentions*

Often we end up doing that which we most tried to avoid. I remember the wife of Ambassador Dwight Morrow telling a story about when her daughters were very small girls. Mrs. Morrow gave a high tea at which one of the guests was to be J. P. Morgan. The girls were to be brought in, introduced, and ushered out. Mrs. Morrow's great fear was the possibility that Anne, the most outspoken, might comment upon Mr. Morgan's bulbous and conspicuous nose. She therefore took pains to explain to Anne that personal observations were impolite, and to caution her especially against making any comment upon Mr. Morgan's nose, no matter what she might think of it. When the moment came and the children were brought in, Mrs. Morrow held her breath as she saw Anne's gaze unfalteringly fix upon this objective and remain there. Nonetheless, the introduction was made, the little girls curtsied and were sent on their way. With a sigh of relief Mrs. Morrow turned back to her duties as hostess and said to her chief guest, "And now, Mr. Morgan, will you have cream or lemon in your nose?"

And similarly sometimes the mistake we most try to avoid is the one we end up making. Today it was my intention to give real recognition to one guest, yet this was the one name I failed to introduce . . .

Mistake—*Perfection*

Unlike some, I don't claim perfection. I admit to human error. Some years ago Secretary of Defense Robert McNamara was resented for the way he and his small band of "Whiz Kids" shunned advice. People grudgingly admitted that McNamara's cost-effectiveness program had brought rationality to much Pentagon planning, but they could not forgive him for never admitting he was wrong. He was once summoned to appear before the House Armed Services Committee to explain why he had ordered the closing of 672 Army bases. Could he have made a mistake in the case of one or two? asked Representative Edward Hébert. "No," said McNamara emphatically. Replied an exasperated Hérbert, "Six hundred and seventy-two decisions and not a single mistake. You're better than Jesus Christ. He had only twelve decisions to make and he blew one of them."

Well, I may blow it too in regard to . . .

Moderator—*Referee*

A stranger accosted Giants Manager John McGraw one afternoon while on the way to the ball park. "What do you want?" barked the man known as Little Napoleon. "How about a pass for today's game?" asked the stranger. "Why should I give you a pass?" asked McGraw. "I'm a friend of the umpire, Bill Klem," answered the other. "No pass!" snapped the Giants manager. "Why not?" asked the stranger. "Because you're a liar!" shouted McGraw. "No umpire ever had a friend."

Well, in this case, I assure you, this umpire or moderator has many friends . . .

Music—*Regulations*

We can get entangled by our own regulations however well meant or intended. Leopold Stokowski was conducting the Philadelphia Orchestra in the Leonore Overture No. 3, which contains a famous offstage trumpet call, and both times the offstage call didn't sound on cue. As soon as the performance ended, Stokowski rushed into the wings, ready to give the delinquent trumpet player a tongue lashing, and found the fellow struggling in the arms of a burly watchman. "I tell you, you can't blow that damn thing in here," the watchman was saying, "there's a concert going on!"

Name—*Courage*

Some names will forever stand out—symbols of enduring human qualities. The black leader Whitney Young once asked Jackie Robinson, Jr., what it was like to be the son of such a famous man. Young Jackie replied, "He has given me a legacy that means much more than wealth or rank—he has given me a name that means courage and guts."

Nature—*Environment*

One of the great ecclesiastics of all time, Saint Bernard, the twelfth-century abbot of Clairvaux, was asked by another cleric what he should read for guidance. Saint Bernard wrote in his return letter: "You will find something far greater in the woods than you will find in books. Stones and trees will teach you that which you will never learn from masters. Think you not you can suck honey from the rock and oil from the desert? Do not the mountains run with sweetness, the hills run with milk and honey and the valleys stand thick with corn?"

Let us today look to our earth, our waters, our minerals, for the lessons they teach us about the way we live . . .

Need—*Lack*

In the Cheshire Cheese pub on Fleet Street old Sam Johnson was told that Richard Brinsley Sheridan was indignant at the lack of interest in his parliamentary speeches and that he had threatened to go to America. Johnson said, "I hope he will go to America." Replied Boswell, "The Americans don't lack oratory." Johnson said, "But we can comfortably lack Sheridan."

Well, there is one person we in this organization we would sorely miss . . .

Needs—*Problems*

There are needs and there are vital priorities necessary to live and survive. I am reminded of the late Senator Henry Fountain Ashurst of Arizona and his maiden speech in the Senate. "Mr. President," Ashurst began, "the baby state I represent has the greatest potential. This state could become a paradise. We need only two things—water and lots of good people." A senior Senator from Pennsylvania, Boies Penrose, interrupted, "If the Senator will pardon me for saying so, that's all they need in hell."

Well, unlike hell, we don't need water but we do need some good men and some capital . . .

Negativism—*Salesmanship*

To sell you must believe in yourself and in what you are selling. For example, when Stonewall Jackson outlined a battle strategy to capture a certain enemy stronghold in northern Virginia his advisers demurred, saying, "I am afraid . . . I fear that . . ." Sternly, Jackson told them, "Never take counsel of your fears."

So let us rather take counsel in our own faith . . .

News—*Communication*

Too many in their frustration confuse the messengers of news with the agents of news. For example, Czar Peter the Great, in 1700, strangled the messengers who came to St. Petersburg to announce the defeat of the Russian fleet by the Swedes at Narva.

Nostalgia—*Youth*

One day, dining at the home of artist Sir Joshua Reynolds, Dr. Samuel Johnson pontificated his gradation of liquors—"claret for boys, port for men, and brandy for heroes." Then said the politician Edmund Burke: "Give me claret for I would love to be a boy and return to the careless gaiety of my youth."

All of us would like to return to the bright, rosy time of childhood . . .

Objections—*Proposal*

As far as I am concerned, the proposal still remains objectionable. There have been some changes, but the substance reminds me of some editing Eugene O'Neill once did. At the tryout of *Ah, Wilderness!* the curtain fell so late that O'Neill was asked to shorten the play. The proud and stubborn O'Neill was adamant about deleting even a word. Finally Russell Crouse was asked to have a word with him. O'Neill liked Crouse and agreed to try. The next morning O'Neill phoned Crouse and said, "You'll be happy to learn I cut fifteen minutes." Crouse could scarcely believe it.

"How?" he asked. "Where did you do it? I'll be right over to get the changes." "There aren't any changes in the text," said O'Neill, "but you know we've been playing this thing in four acts. I've decided to cut out the third intermission."

Objectivity—*Faults*

Alexander the Great engaged an artist to paint his portrait. He set down only two conditions: it was to be an exact likeness, unfalsified, and it was to be handsome and attractive. The artist was confronted with a painful dilemma, however, for over his right eye Alexander had a prominent battle scar. To omit the scar would be a violation of the first condition; to include it would be a violation of the second. Finally, the artist decided to paint Alexander in a pensive mood, his head supported by his right hand with his forefinger covering the scar.

Well, we all would like to cover up our faults and deficiencies, but in our own hearts we are aware of them . . .

Observation—*Details*

Dr. Billroth, the famous Viennese surgeon, told his students that a doctor needed two abilities: freedom from nausea and power of observation. Then he dipped his finger into a bitterly foul fluid and licked it off, requesting them to do the same. They did it without flinching. With a grin, Dr. Billroth said, "You have passed the first test well, but not the second, for none of you noticed that I dipped my first finger in the liquid but licked the second."

Well, in the recent publicity you have followed the appearance of things without perceiving the true facts . . .

Observer—*Bench*

The immortal Knute Rockne used to hold skull sessions with his players that were as sharp and demanding of them as any mathematical quiz. It was Rockne's custom to fling out complicated questions in strategy and demand immediate answers from his Notre Damers. One afternoon, Rockne shot out this question at his third-string quarterback: "Our ball, third quarter, second down,

two yards to go and we're at mid-field. What do you do?" "Me?"
asked the startled third-stringer. "I just slide down the bench to
get a better look at the next play!"

Well, as one who was not a participant in the recent struggle,
I'm not going to second-guess . . .

Obsession—*One-Track*

President Ulysses S. Grant had no ear for music. One time during
a concert at Peabody Institute in Baltimore he turned to Robert
Winthrop, sitting next to him, and said, "Why, Mr. Winthrop, I
know only two tunes. One is 'Yankee Doodle' and the other isn't."

And our demagogic friend knows only two political tunes—one
is law and order and the other is not . . .

Obvious—*Inference*

One day Sir Arthur Conan Doyle arrived in Paris and asked a cab
driver to take him to a certain hotel. The cab driver, recognizing
his passenger as the famous creator of Sherlock Holmes, said, "I
perceive, sir, that you have recently visited Constantinople and
there are strong indications you have been in the neighborhood
of Milan. I further deduce that you have recently been in Budapest."

"Wonderful! Very clever! I'll give you five francs extra if you tell
me how you arrived at so accurate a conclusion," said the great
author of detective fiction. "It was easy," said the cab driver
proudly, "I simply looked at the labels on your luggage."

And if we look closely, we can perceive some indications . . .

Offense—*Attack*

In the 1950s the New York Giants' football coach Allie Sherman,
during one of his team's less successful seasons, was late for a
football luncheon at a hotel. He darted through a revolving door
with such speed that he upended an old dignified gentleman in
his path who happened to be heading for the same luncheon.
"No offense, sir," apologized coach Sherman. "You're telling
me!" roared the old duffer, who happened to be a loyal Giants

fan. "That's been your trouble all year long."

Well, in a sense, the business community has remained on the defensive too long . . .

Offering—*Token*

When Alexander Woollcott moved into a new apartment, he announced to his friends that he would anticipate from them a shower of gifts. "Actually," he said, "I would appreciate your sending me china, linen, and silver." Accordingly, F. P. Adams had delivered to the apartment a moustache cup, a handkerchief, and a dime.

Well, in this cause none of our hearts will be satisfied with such a token commitment . . .

Office—*Humility*

When Harry Truman became President, Sam Rayburn took him aside to give him some advice: "From here on out you're going to have lots of people around you. They'll try to put a wall around you and cut you off from any ideas but theirs. They'll tell you what a great man you are, Harry. But you and I both know you ain't."

Well, I'm still the same man I always was—which my wife will attest to . . .

Office—*Remoteness*

As I assume this new position I think of some wise words of Cardinal Francis Spellman. When he became Archbishop of the New York Diocese he turned to his secretary and said, "Oh my, it looks like I shall never again eat a poor meal or hear the truth."

If this dinner is any indication, I am already seeing part of his prophecy come true. I only hope you who are my friends won't let the other thing happen and that you will tell me the truth—when I am wrong and when I can do better . . .

Opinion—*Criticism*

I don't mind criticism, but I do think you have to examine the source. Once when George Bernard Shaw was making a curtain speech, he was interrupted by a strident voice from the gallery that said, "Shut up, Shaw. Your play is rotten!" "You and I know that," Shaw replied, "but who are we among so many?"

So I would say that one lone but vocal critic . . .

Opportunity—*Challenge*

The challenge that awaits reminds me of the ancient coat of arms of the royal family of Spain. Before Columbus set sail to cross the Atlantic, it was believed that the world ended out there somewhere past Gibraltar. To the Spanish, one of their real glories was that they were the last outpost of the world, and that their country fronted right on the great beyond. Therefore the royal coat of arms showed the Pillars of Hercules, the great columns guarding the Strait of Gibraltar, and the royal motto said plainly *Ne Plus Ultra*, meaning, roughly, "there is no more beyond here."

But then, when Columbus returned, he had actually discovered a whole new world out there. The ancient motto was now meaningless. In this crisis someone at Court made a noble and thrifty suggestion, which was immediately bought by Queen Isabella. It was simply that the first word, *Ne*, be deleted. Now the motto on the coat of arms read—and has read ever since—just two words: *Plus Ultra*—"There is plenty more beyond."

Opportunity—*Patronage*

The problem with government is that too often only those with connections are offered jobs. Abraham Lincoln understood this. A woman with a commanding air once addressed him thus: "Mr. President, you must give me a colonel's commission for my son. I demand it of you, sir, not as a favor but as a right. My grandfathers fought at Lexington; my uncle was the only man who did not run at Bladensburg; my father fought at New Orleans, and my husband was killed at Monterey." "I guess, madam," said Lincoln, "your family has done enough for our country. It's time to give somebody else a chance."

Opportunity—*Timing*

When an opportunity presents itself, you must seize it. Voltaire, the French writer and philosopher, might never have become known if he hadn't taken advantage of a bureaucratic mistake. A brilliant mathematician, he saw an obvious miscalculation in the government issuance of a national lottery. Forming a syndicate, he bought up every ticket. His share made him independently comfortable and gave him time to write.

Optimism—*Difficulties*

Robert Louis Stevenson was ill with tuberculosis the greater part of his life. One day his wife went into his room when he had been compelled to put aside his manuscript to stanch the lifeblood that he was coughing away. "I suppose you will tell me that it is a glorious day," she said. "Yes," he replied as he looked at the sunlight streaming through his window. "I refuse to permit a row of medicine bottles to block the horizon."

So after listening to a litany of our many problems, let's, for a change, look at the bright side . . .

Optimism—*Predictions*

James Boswell wrote how Samuel Johnson once met an old college companion, Oliver Edwards, whom he had not seen for nearly fifty years. During the course of their talk Edwards remarked naïvely, "You are a philosopher, Dr. Johnson; I have tried too in my time to be a philosopher, but, I don't know how, cheerfulness was always breaking in."

But tradition notwithstanding, I am going to be optimistic in my predictions . . .

Options—*Choice*

Though there are available a few options, each one is fraught with difficulty. In that sense I am like Chief Quannah Parker. In his old age, after he quit the warpath, Quannah Parker, the famous chief of the Comanches, adopted many of the white man's ways. But in one respect he clung to the custom of his fathers. He continued to be a polygamist. He was a friend and admirer of Theodore Roosevelt and on one occasion when Roosevelt was touring Oklahoma he drove out to Parker's camp to see him. With pride Parker pointed out that he lived in a house like a white man, his children went to a white man's school, and he himself dressed like a white man. Whereupon Roosevelt was moved to preach him a sermon on the subject of morality. "See here, chief, why don't you set your people a better example? A white man has only one wife—he's allowed only one at a time. Here you are living with five squaws. Why don't you give up four of them and remain faithful to the fifth?" Parker stood still a moment, considering the proposition. Then he answered, "You are my great white father, and I will do as you wish—on one condition." "What is the condition?" asked Roosevelt. "You pick out the one I am to live with and then you go kill the other four," answered Parker.

Outmatched—*Warning*
Once during a tense, rough, and brawling hockey game, courageous Camille Henry, one of the tiniest players in the National Hockey League, lost his temper and tangled with big tough defenseman Fernie Flaman, one of the most feared sluggers in the league. As they grappled, shoulder to shoulder, pint-sized Henry suddenly shouted a warning at his huge opponent, who outweighed him by more than seventy pounds: "Watch out, Fernie, or I'll bleed all over you!"

Oversell—*Prolixity*
Salesmanship is a matter of timing. Without it, selling can become overselling. Mark Twain understood this. He was attending a meeting where a missionary had been invited to speak. Twain was deeply impressed. Later he said, "The preacher's voice was beautiful. He told us about the sufferings of the natives, and he pleaded for help with such moving simplicity that I mentally doubled the fifty cents I had intended to put in the plate. He described the pitiful misery of those savages so vividly that the dollar I had in

mind gradually rose to five. Then that preacher continued, and I felt that all the cash I carried on me would be insufficient, and I decided to write a large check. Then he went on," added Twain. "He went on and on and on about the dreadful state of those natives and I abandoned the idea of the check. And he went on. And I got back to five dollars. And he went on, and I got back to four, two, one. And still he went on. And when the plate came around . . . I took ten cents out of it."

Pacifists—*Realists*

In 1966, when the United States embarked on a policy of bombing the oil depots in North Vietnam, thus "escalating" the war, many liberals and intellectuals raised their voices in opposition to the administration's military policy. A substantial few, however, supported the government's stand. Among those who agreed with President Johnson was Dr. John Roche, professor of political science at Brandeis University, a keen scholar and provocative, liberal thinker on most matters. One day, Dr. Roche was lecturing on the necessity for our participation in the hostilities when a student interrupted his talk. "Would Christ have carried a draft card?" shouted the heckler. And Dr. Roche countered, "Would Christ have carried a social security card?"

Partisanship—*Politics*

Once Congressman Thaddeus Stevens went into the room of the Committee on Elections, of which he was a member, and found a hearing going on. He asked one of his Republican colleagues what was the point in the case. "There isn't much point to it," was the answer. "They are both damned scoundrels." "Well," said Stevens, "which is the Republican damned scoundrel? I want to be for the Republican damned scoundrel."

It is that type of narrow partisanship that clogs the legislative process . . .

Party—*Fellowship*

I would like to close this meeting with a comment by Winston Churchill. He was presiding over a cabinet meeting when an aide informed him that the Archbishop of Canterbury, some years his junior, had died. Churchill was able to restrain his grief at the news. "You see," he said to his cabinet members, "a total abstainer dead of gout. It just proves how right my habits are."

Well, let us now, like Churchill, indulge in some of those habits that insure a longevity . . .

Pastor—*Doctor*

When I see the good reverend doctor here at the head table I am reminded of an occasion when Norman Vincent Peale, the famous preacher, once made use of the services of a young physician who was not an ardent churchgoer. Subsequently the doctor never sent a bill. "Look here, doctor," Peale said finally, "I have to know how much I owe you." After thinking it over, the physician said, "I'll tell you, Dr. Peale: I hear you're a pretty fair preacher, and you seem to think I'm a pretty good doctor. I'll make a bargain with you. I'll do all I can to keep you out of heaven, if you'll do all you can to keep me out of hell, and it won't cost either of us a cent."

Well, as a lawyer I tried to make a similar deal, but the good doctor said he had much the harder job . . .

Patience—*Practice*

An admirer once asked pianist Ignace Paderewski, "Is it true that you still practice every day?" "Yes," said the pianist. "At least six hours a day." "You must have a world of patience," said the other. "I have no more patience than the next fellow," said Paderewski. "I just use mine."

Pause—*Adjournment*

As I look at the hour, I want to make sure I don't make the mistake General Eisenhower once did. It was in 1952 when the general headed the NATO military command near Paris. His old wartime colleague Winston Churchill had been re-elected prime minister in late 1951 and had scheduled an inspection tour of the NATO defenses.

Ike's deputy, Al Gruenther, in preparation for the luncheon visit, had suggested that they lay in some fine old cognac. On the day of the visit the rare cognac they had acquired was poured into a Baccarat decanter and placed on the Louis Seize sideboard in the dining room of the Allied Commander's residence.

The lunch, which was something of a reunion, went well. But Eisenhower, whose back was to the sideboard, had completely forgotten the special refreshment of spirit he had provided for the occasion.

All at once in the midst of some discussion about German troops, Churchill said, "Ike, that certainly is a splendid sideboard. Where did you get it?"

Ike, despite kicks by Gruenther, muttered something about their inheriting the piece when the château was leased by NATO and then went back to his monologue about German troops.

Then Churchill said, "Ike, that certainly is an exquisite carafe on the sideboard."

"Oh," said Ike, "Al picked that up in Paris. It is beautiful, isn't it?"

"Yes," said Churchill, "but not as beautiful as what's inside it. Can't you see that I am thirsty."

Well, similarly, I think all of us could stand some liquid refreshment . . .

Peace—*Negotiation*

In the late 1940s Dr. Robert Oppenheimer, the Princeton scientist, was called to testify before the Senate Armed Services Committee. As a member of the Manhattan Project that was responsible for the creation of the atom bomb, Dr. Oppenheimer was asked this question: "Doctor, is there any defense against such a nuclear weapon?" "Certainly," he replied. "What is that, Doctor?" And Dr. Oppenheimer replied, "Peace."

In this nuclear age we can't afford *not* to explore means of arms control . . .

Peace—*Urgency*

In 1962 Norman Cousins, editor of the *Saturday Review*, journeyed to Rome to interview Pope John XXIII. During his audience at the Vatican, he asked Pope John, "What do you think the world needs most?" Pope John replied, "World peace is mankind's greatest need. I am old but I will do what I can in the time I have."

Perfection—*Beauty*

In presenting the next honoree, I can say she is as talented as she is beautiful. It doesn't always work out that way. When Sir Thomas Beecham conducted opera at Covent Garden, the sopranos were more on the robust side. He was once asked why he did not choose sopranos who ate less. "I would like to," sighed Beecham, who had an eye for a shapely female, "but unfortunately those who sing like birds eat like horses—and vice versa."

Perfection—*Creativity*

After completing his statue of Moses, the Renaissance sculptor Michelangelo surveyed his work and then struck in anger the knee of the masterpiece, crying, "Why dost thou not speak?"

It was Michelangelo's compulsive search for divine perfection that fueled his artistic drive . . .

Perfection—*Humanity*

One afternoon in St. Louis, Stan ("The Man") Musial was having a field day against the Chicago pitcher, crusty Bobo Newsom. Stan first slammed a single, then a triple, and then a homer. When Stan came up to bat for the fourth time, the Chicago manager, Charlie Grimm, decided to yank Bobo and take a chance on a rookie relief pitcher. The rookie trudged in from the bullpen and took the ball from Bobo. "Say," he murmured, "has this guy Musial got any weaknesses?" "Yeah," grunted Bobo, "he can't hit doubles."

And if our friend has any weakness it is that he can't say no to someone in need—he can't hit anyone when he is down . . .

Perfection—*Remembrance*

When Cy Young, the winningest pitcher in baseball whose life-time mark of 511 triumphs will never be surpassed, was over eighty years old he was approached by a young sports reporter. Cy answered all the eager lad's questions willingly. "Just one more, Mr. Young," said the young reporter finally. "What was your favorite pitch when you had the bases full behind you?" "My boy," Young replied with a perfectly straight face, "I don't recall ever having to pitch with the bases full."

Like Cy Young, some of us, in looking back, tend to forget the rough spots . . .

Perfection—*Retouching*

In the Great Hall of Chequers, where the British Prime Minister resides, hangs an old masterpiece by the Flemish painter Peter Paul Rubens. It illustrates the fable of the lion caught in a net and the mouse that freed him by gnawing the bonds. The painting has been admired by a succession of prime ministers. But something about the Rubens mouse jarred Sir Winston Churchill's artistic sensibilities. The mouse seemed too small for the thick ropes. Finally, Churchill, an amateur painter himself, could stand it no longer. He called for his brush and easel, and determinedly re-touched the mouse in the masterpiece.

Perhaps a Churchill can add touches to a Rubens but the rest of us should let a masterpiece stand . . .

Perfection—*Worry*

If you do your best, you shouldn't worry. You shouldn't worry about what you can't change. This is what Noel Coward meant when he wrote a postcard to his friend David Niven, the actor. The urbane Niven is, offstage, a very intense striver for perfection. The card Coward sent him showed the Venus de Milo, and the message read: "You see what will happen to you if you keep on biting your nails."

Performance—*Rotten*

When tough Herman Hickman was football coach at Yale University he would become so upset at times that he would forget to mind his best Ivy League manners. One afternoon, his Yale team was locked in a fierce grid battle against its traditional rival, Princeton. Suddenly, the referee gave the signal for a costly penalty against Yale. Coach Hickman blew his top, for that penalty nullified a long touchdown run. As the referee paced off the penalty yardage, a furious Hickman ran along the sidelines yelling angrily: "Hey, ref, what team are you on, anyway? It's hard enough to beat Princeton without having the referee playing for them. You stink! You stink!" The referee promptly slapped another penalty against Yale, and paced off an additional fifteen yards. Then he turned around and said sweetly to the speechless Yale coach, "How do I smell to you from here, Mr. Hickman?"

Well, gentlemen, from my distance and perspective the performance we have been witnessing the last few years . . .

Performance—*Tie*

Although I am not unhappy with the results, I feel somewhat like the late Eddie Erdelatz, the Naval Academy football coach in the 1950s. When his team played West Point to a 7–7 tie Eddie was asked his reaction. "A tie game," he said, "is like kissing your sister."

So let us give two cheers for the performance and get back to work . . .

Permissiveness—*Character*

Not long ago Katharine Hepburn was being interviewed by a reporter from *People* magazine. Miss Hepburn expressed her distaste for the increasing permissiveness in a society where character and moral strength were no longer emulated ideals. The journalist asked, "Miss Hepburn, do you think that this era will pass?" "Yes," replied Hepburn. "The pendulum will begin to swing back, but someone has to begin by giving it a push."

We have a chance to give that pendulum a shove today by standing up for . . .

Permissiveness—*Discipline*

Samuel Taylor Coleridge, the great English poet of the Romantic period, was once talking with a man who told him that he did not believe in giving children any religious instruction whatsoever. His theory was that the child's mind should not be prejudiced in any direction, but when he came to years of discretion he should be permitted to choose his religious opinions for himself. Coleridge said nothing, but after a while he asked his visitor if he would like to see his garden. The man said he would and Coleridge took him out into the garden, where only weeds were growing. The man looked at Coleridge in surprise, and said, "Why, this is not a garden! There are nothing but weeds here!" "Well, you see," answered Coleridge, "I did not wish to infringe upon the liberty of the garden in any way. I was just giving the garden a chance to express itself and to choose its own production."

Perseverance—*Excellence*

Though talent may be born, perfection is only had by constant practice and perseverance. A great pianist once played to an audience of titled people, performing a sonata so brilliantly the listeners could hardly believe it. The conclusion of the piece was followed by an instant of breathless silence—then thunderous applause. It was the Queen of England who stepped forward to say, "Mr. Paderewski, you are a genius." Bowing gravely, Paderewski replied, "Before I became a genius, Your Majesty, I was a drudge."

Persistence—*Conviction*

When the fall of the Confederacy was at hand, General Grant invited President Lincoln to come down to visit him at his headquarters at City Point on the James River. As they sat that night around the campfire, Lincoln related some of his characteristic anecdotes, and then sat in silence, looking into the fire.

Grant looked up and said, "Mr. President, did you at any time doubt the final success of the cause?" Straightening himself up in his camp chair, and leaning forward and lifting his hand by way of emphasis, Lincoln replied with great solemnity, "Never, for a moment!"

And I don't doubt for a moment the success of our cause . . .

Perspective—*Planning*

Michelangelo, the great painter of the Italian Renaissance, once looked over one of Raphael's sketches and wrote under it, "Amplius," which means "greater," or "expand." Raphael's layout in Michelangelo's opinion, was too cramped and narrow.

Sometimes we don't look at a larger perspective—we don't see the big picture . . .

Perspective—*Provincialism*

There are places in this world where my remarks might be misunderstood—not because others lack understanding, but because our ways are not always the ways of others. Much of what we think and do would prove strange in other lands. Americans don't always recognize this.

Donald Swann, the actor, tells about the Indian he sat next to on a flight from Fiji to Calcutta who was completely baffled by the breakfast served on their jet. First, he poured his coffee into the cornflakes and ate them. Then he mixed the milk and the sugar and drank it. Next, he licked the butter from the small square of paper. And for a chaser, he ate the marmalade.

Perspective—*Viewpoint*

When Robert Benchley was a student at Harvard he took a course in international law. The final examination confronted him with a question something like this: Discuss the arbitration of the international fisheries problem with respect to hatcheries protocol and dragnet and trawl procedure as it affects (a) the point of view of the United States and (b) the point of view of Great Britain.

Benchley, who had not studied, was somewhat desperate, and

wrote as follows: "I know nothing about the point of view of Great Britain in the arbitration of the international fisheries problem, and nothing about the point of view of the United States. Therefore, I shall discuss the question from the point of view of the fish."

Well, today I would like to analyze a well-known problem from a different perspective . . .

⇥

Claude Monet, one of France's most renowned painters of the nineteenth century, was able to paint the same object a dozen times, at different hours of the day. Each time it would appear different to him because of the new shades of light and accentuation that the time of day and the seasons of the year would bring to it. He painted some twenty pictures of the west façade of Rouen Cathedral, at twenty sequent times of day, and the color and appearance of each brought an entirely new and refreshing view.

If you stand close to one of these pictures, it will look like frosting on a cake dotted with color. From a bit farther back, it looks like a colorful but confusing jigsaw puzzle. Stand still farther back and the full beauty of the cathedral comes into view with its imposing arches and towers.

Similarly, our attitude toward life is dictated by the perspectives and insights we have gained, which are but a reflection of the type and amount of light we allow to shine upon it.

Piety—*Humility*

During the Civil War a delegation of Methodist clergymen called on President Lincoln. Their spokesman said to the President, "I know the Lord is on our side." The President instantly replied, "I am not concerned about that, for I know the Lord is always on the side of the right. But it is my constant anxiety and prayer that I and this nation should be on the Lord's side."

Lincoln was gently reminding his callers that it borders on impiety as well as intolerance to arrogate the name of the Lord to one's own cause. Rather, we should be ever asking ourselves: "Are we doing the Lord's work?"

Piousness—*Compromise*

A Boston parishioner seeking to impress Cardinal Richard Cushing with his piety was bemoaning the fact that there seem to be so few saints among us in this materialistic twentieth century. "Well, let's all give thanks for that," said the eminent cardinal. "Saints are all right in heaven, but they're hell on earth."

What His Eminence meant was that self-appointed guardians are usually a pain in the ass . . .

Plagiarism—*Assessment*

My reaction to the State of the Union address is much the same as that of Dr. Samuel Johnson when he commented on an essay by a protégé. He told the student: "I found your speech to be good and original. However, the part that was original was not good. And the part that was good was not original."

Planning—*Compensation*

During his ball-playing prime Hank Greenberg demanded a fancy salary from Walter Briggs, then owner of the Detroit Tigers. "I don't see why you want so much money, Hank," said Briggs. "When I was your age I had two children and was earning $25 a week." "That's why I want so much now," said Greenberg. "When I'm your age I may have two children and be earning $25 a week."

Similarly, all of us must look ahead and plan for future needs . . .

Planning—*Delay*

I think we might be underestimating the time needed for organizing such an operation. It reminds me of what Winston Churchill said to Franklin Roosevelt in World War II. Churchill was always more aware of the potential danger of the Russian allies than F.D.R. was. When the Yalta Conference was proposed, F.D.R. was already too ill to fight Stalin point by point and expressed a hope that the meeting should last at most five or six days.

In a memo to Roosevelt, Churchill wrote: "I do not see any way of realizing our hopes about a world organization in five or six days, even the Almighty took seven."

Planning—*Investment*

George Eastman, captain of Kodak, had always had a genius for detail. After looking over the architect's plan for a theater with six thousand seats which he was planning to give to the city of Rochester, New York, Mr. Eastman indicated general approval, but thought there was room for two more seats in the orchestra. "Why raise the issue about two seats when there are six thousand in the theater?" queried the architect. And Eastman is reported to have replied: "Each extra seat, for which there is ample room, would bring in an additional revenue of thirty cents a show, making sixty cents for the day, or $3.60 a week, figuring six performances. At the end of the year, the revenue would amount to $187.20, which, incidentally, is the interest on $3,120 for a year."

Similarly, we should look and see whether we are maximizing our return . . .

Planning—*Research*

In 1926 a chemical director of a great industrial plant had a novel idea which would revolutionize business. The man was Dr. Charles Stone and he wrote a letter to the company president, Lammot Du Pont, asking for a $30,000 allotment for basic research. The suggestion was unheard of. But his words persuaded Du Pont. "Fundamental research is not a labor of love—it is a sound business policy that should assure the payment of future dividends."

In other words, research is not the dessert but the first course for any great business . . .

Platitudes—*Programs*

What has been said so far in this conference is best described by some words of the late Mayor Richard Daley when he dedicated a cornerstone in Chicago. Inadvertently he proclaimed, "Together we must rise to higher and higher platitudes."

I think the time has come to fit programs to our principles . . .

Poetry—*Sensitivity*

Socialist intellectual Beatrice Webb couldn't understand poetry. She once told novelist Arnold Bennett, "Poetry means nothing to me. It confuses me. I always want to translate it back into prose."

Fortunately not all intellectuals lack sensitivity . . .

Poise—*Emergency*

During the Cleveland presidency, a young second secretary from the Swedish embassy at a White House dinner cut into a wedge of lettuce and found a live worm. He was about to push the plate away when he noticed Mrs. Cleveland watching him intently. He stiffened in his chair and then ate the lettuce, worm and all.

"That wasn't necessary," said Mrs. Cleveland, "but it showed fantastic poise in time of emergency—you will go far, young man."

Fifteen years later, he was back as his country's ambassador in Washington.

Politics—*Choice*

Norman Thomas ran for President six times on the Socialist Party ticket. During the 1944 election, a G.I. who didn't know him asked him whom he was voting for, and Thomas replied that he was voting for himself. This stopped the G.I. cold until Thomas explained that he was the Socialist candidate for the presidency. The G.I. thought that over a moment, then said, "Well, if you weren't running who would you vote for?"

Well, in a similar spirit, I would choose . . .

Politics—*Government*

When I am asked why I don't retire, I am reminded of what Winston Churchill said to a young man who cornered him after a political meeting. "Sir Winston," he asked, "what prompted you to get into politics?" "Ambition, my son," the sage old statesman answered, "pure unadulterated ambition." "What made you stay in politics?" he asked. "Anger," Churchill replied, "pure adulterated anger."

Politics—*Legislation*

Once a group of university students went to observe the proceedings of the French Assembly. They were disgusted at the pompous exchanges and the empty rhetoric. All of a sudden they noted a strange, ugly man watching them intently and laughing. "Why are you laughing, Monsieur?" one said. "I am laughing at your naïveté," said Count Mirabeau. "Laws are like sausages. You should never see them made."

And I think if we had actually seen some of the manipulation by special interests and pressure by certain lobbies we would have been sickened . . .

Politics—*Reason*

My reasons for taking this action are much like those of General Grant in the 1856 presidential election. Convinced that a victory for Frémont would cause a rebellion in the slave states, Grant voted for Buchanan, and commented: "I voted for Buchanan because I didn't know him and voted against Frémont because I did know him."

Politics—*Rhetoric*

The cant of politics is bad but it is even worse when it is wrapped in the black cloth of clerical pieties. For example, Stanley Baldwin, prime minister of Britain in the 1920s, always liked to frame his speeches with spiritual references for the homey touch. When he was going over with the cabinet the speech he was subsequently to make in the House of Commons upon the accession of King Edward VIII, his secretary gathered up the manuscript and observed a marginal note by the prime minister: "Refer again to A. G." Promptly the speech was rushed to the attorney-general. The hour was late and in some puzzlement the A. G. and his staff scrutinized the wholly innocuous phrases, wondering what Mr. Baldwin could possibly have thought might be indiscreet or dangerous. It turned out next morning that the prime minister had meant to remind himself by his marginal note to "Refer again to Almighty God."

Posterity—*God*

Shortly before he died, the French philosopher Voltaire predicted from his Swiss home that in one hundred years the Bible would be a forgotten book, found only in museums. When the one hundred years were up, Voltaire's home was occupied by the Geneva Bible Society.

Although it is sometimes difficult to know what is ephemeral and what is lasting, we know that what we are developing today will be enjoyed by posterity. That which is spiritual and educational is more enduring than the material . . .

Poverty—*Humanity*

One of the greatest mayors New York ever had was Fiorello La-Guardia—"the Little Flower." Many older New Yorkers remember the day Fiorello read the funny papers over the radio—with all the appropriate excitement and inflections—when a strike kept the Sunday journals off the stands. They remember, too, his squeaky outbursts against the "crooks" and "bums" who would exploit the poor. One time the ubiquitous mayor chose to preside in a night court. It was bitter cold outside. An old lady was brought before him, charged with stealing a loaf of bread. Her family, she said, was starving. "I've got to punish you," declared LaGuardia. "The law makes no exceptions. I must fine you ten dollars." But the mayor added as he was reaching into his own pocket, "Well, here's the ten dollars to pay your fine—which I now remit." He tossed the ten-dollar bill into his famous sombrero. "Furthermore," he declared, "I'm going to fine everybody in this courtroom fifty cents for living in a town where a person has to steal bread in order to eat. Mr. Bailiff, collect the fines and give them to this defendant!"

The hat was passed and an incredulous old lady, with a light of heaven in her eyes, left the courtroom with a stake of $47.50.

And the question is, what can we do to lighten the burdens of those more unfortunate than ourselves . . .

Poverty—*Realism*

Once Pope Julius II criticized Michelangelo for his ceiling of the Sistine Chapel. He suggested that the artist put a gilding around where the prophets were depicted or it would look poor. Replied Michelangelo, "The people I painted were poor."

Today we must not paint an idealized picture of our society . . .

Power—*Risk*

When Maximilian left Vienna to assume the throne in Mexico, the Archduchess Sophia said to her son, "Remember, my child, one does not descend from a throne except to mount a scaffold." The emperor was executed less than a year later.

There is no greater fall than that of the powerful . . .

Practicality—*Planning*

I think we should confine our planning to the more practical aspects. I am reminded of the time G. K. Chesterton and several other literary figures were asked one evening what book they would prefer to have with them if stranded on a desert isle. "The complete works of Shakespeare," said one writer without hesitation. "I'd choose the Bible," interrupted another. "How about you?" someone asked Chesterton. "I would choose," replied the portly author, *"Thomas's Guide to Practical Shipbuilding."*

Predictions—*Success*

During a conversation in 1864 on the approaching presidential election, a friend asked President Lincoln what if Grant's capture of Richmond was followed by his nomination and acceptance of the candidacy. "Well," said Lincoln, "I feel very much like the man who said he didn't want to die particularly, but if he had to die, that was precisely the disease he would like to die of."

Similarly, if my predictions are proved to be wrong, I would only be too happy . . .

Prejudice—*Brotherhood*

In the days before the Civil War, Wendell Phillips was accosted on a lecture tour by a minister who hailed from the state of Kentucky, a place with views very different from those of the abolitionists. The clergyman, who was more militant on behalf of his prejudices than on behalf of his creed, said, "You're Wendell Phillips, I believe." "Yes, I am." "You want to free the blacks, don't you?" "Yes, I do." "Well, why do you preach your doctrines up North? Why don't you try coming down to Kentucky?" Phillips began to counter-question the man. "You're a preacher, are you not?" "Yes, I am, sir." "Are you trying to save souls from hell?" "Why yes, sir. That is my business." "Why don't you go there then?" replied Phillips.

And that is not a bad suggestion for those who would pervert the ideals of our Declaration of Independence and subvert the Constitution . . .

Prejudice—*Fear*

You fear and hate only what you don't know and understand. Once when the English essayist Charles Lamb was talking at length against someone, his companion said, "Did you ever meet him, Charles?" "No, I don't know him. I don't hate anyone I know."

Isn't that the root of all prejudice—fearing and hating what we don't know or take the time to understand . . .

Prepared—*Armed*

During the Lyndon Johnson administration Jack Benny was invited one evening to the White House to play his violin. As he approached the White House a guard stopped him outside the gate and asked, "What do you have in that case, Mr. Benny?" Benny answered solemnly, "A machine gun." With equal solemnity, the guard replied, "Enter. I was afraid for a minute it was your violin!"

Well, our guest has come tonight prepared to . . .

Preparedness—*Contingency*

In any case we should be prepared for either contingency. When Senator Lyndon Johnson, then Democratic majority leader, was in the hospital with his first heart attack, Mrs. Johnson asked him what to do about the two suits he had ordered from the tailor. Mr. Johnson said, "Well, Bird, I guess you better tell him to keep the brown one, but send over the blue one. We'll need the blue one whatever happens."

Preparedness—*Foreign Policy*

In March 1946 when Winston Churchill journeyed to the United States to deliver his famous Iron Curtain speech in Fulton, Missouri, he first stopped at the White House where he was a guest of President Harry Truman.

President Truman showed him the new United States seal he had designed. The eagle holds arrows in one claw and an olive branch in the other. In the old seal the eagle faced the arrows, but Truman by executive order had it changed so that it faced the olive branch. Truman thought that it better reflected the peaceful intention of the United States. When he asked Churchill for his comment, he replied, "Better yet—why not put the eagle's neck on a swivel so that it could turn to the right or left as the occasion presented itself."

Press—*Leak*

One of the most famous leaks to the press necessitated President Lincoln's appearance in front of the House Judiciary Committee. He was asked how a paragraph in his State of the Union Address had reached the New York *Herald* in advance. (There was no official record of the hearing, but the New York *Tribune* reported that a White House gardener had been the leaker!)

Press—*Misquotation*

The press, in its attempted summation of my views, distorted them. I feel the way E. B. White did when he wrote to the *Reader's*

Digest after it had condensed one of his works. White wrote, "Unlike a vanilla bean, I do not want to be extracted."

Press—*Stamina*

When Teddy Roosevelt was Governor of New York, he used to have his theories about interviews. He would run up the seventy-seven steps of the state capitol at Albany every day, followed by the press. Any reporter who finished with him and still had the breath to ask a question would get an answer.

Not only physical stamina is needed by both the press and public officials today . . .

Press—*Vulnerable*

A public official's vulnerability to the press was never better illustrated than by what once happened to President John Quincy Adams back in the 1820s. Behind the White House, in what is now the Ellipse, the old Chesapeake and Potomac Canal used to run before it was filled in. Adams used to skinny-dip there in the early morning as part of his daily regimen. But once an enterprising lady reporter named Anne Royall who had been refused a presidential interview decided to force Adams into changing his mind. He did one morning when she went down to the canal and sat on his clothes he had left on the bank.

Well, the ingenuity of the press has continued, as you can see, unabated, and so has the vulnerability of some officials . . .

Pressure—*Ambition*

In our compulsive drive to succeed, we often override our own values and loyalties. This is true in business as well as politics. We don't want to appear like British Prime Minister Macmillan did in 1962, when in an effort to raise the sagging prestige of the Conservative government, he dismissed a third of the cabinet. In his comment on the wholesale bloodletting, Jeremy Thorpe, a brilliant young Liberal Party member, said, "The Prime Minister has reversed the familiar scriptural injunction to read 'Greater love hath no man than this, that he lay down his friends for his own life.' "

Pressure—*Clutch*

Some years ago one of baseball's most colorful characters, Bobo Newsom, was called into the commissioner's office for being seen at the racetrack. The old commissioner, Judge Kenesaw Mountain Landis, believed that gambling and baseball didn't mix, and lectured baseball's famous roustabout. "Bobo, a ballplayer who bets on racehorses can't keep his mind on the game! Suppose you're pitching in a tight ball game and have to go to bat in the eighth inning when you've got a big bet going on a horse. What will you be thinking of then, baseball or your bet?" Pitcher Newsom looked the tough judge squarely in the eye, and squashed him with a direct and honest reply: "Mr. Commissioner, you don't have to worry about that. If it's a tight ball game in the eighth, it's a sure bet Ol' Bobo won't be in there batting!"

But you can be sure that the man we honor tonight was always one you could depend on when the fight was toughest and the pressure thickest . . .

Problem—*Difficulty*

We have a problem much like the one the poet and playwright William Butler Yeats once described. The prima donna Mrs. Pat Campbell was playing in his *Deirdre*. He described her as having "an ego like a raging tooth" and spoke of her habit of "throwing tantrums" at rehearsals. On one occasion after a particularly wild "tantrum" she walked to the footlights and peered out at Yeats, who was pacing up and down the aisles of the Abbey Theatre. "I'd give anything to know what you're thinking," shouted Mrs. Pat. "I'm thinking," replied Yeats, "of the master of a wayside Indian railway station who sent a message to his company's headquarters saying: 'Tigress on the line: wire instructions.' "

Problem—*Expensive*

It's going to take some money to get out of this mess. We may have to take the route that the famous Hungarian playwright Ferenc

Molnár took on one occasion. Molnár and a friend were presented with two free tickets to a Budapest play. Early in the insufferable first act, Molnár got up to leave. "You can't walk out," objected his companion. "We're guests of the management." Molnár meekly sat down, but after a few more doses of insipid dialogue, he rose again. "Now where are you going?" queried his friend. Said Molnár, "I'm going to the box office to buy two tickets so we can leave."

Problem—*Question*

Before we can propose any solution, we should analyze the problem. When Gertrude Stein was dying, she murmured to a friend who was at her bedside, "What is the answer?" There was silence and then she said: "In that case, what is the question?"

Procedure—*Ingenuity*

When Abraham Lincoln was captain of the "Bucktail" Rangers in 1832 during the Black Hawk war, he was as ignorant of military matters as his company was of drill and tactics. On one occasion his troop, marching in platoon formation, was confronted by a gate. Captain Lincoln had no idea of the proper order, but his quick wit did not desert him. "Company dismissed for two minutes," he commanded. "At the end of that time, fall in and on the other side of the fence."

I think, however, that we must find a way to accomplish our objective working through the proper channels . . .

Procedure—*Protocol*

Once President Calvin Coolidge was having breakfast with the Italian ambassador, and discussing a recent trade agreement. The envoy was somewhat puzzled when the President carefully poured his cup of milk into a saucer but, diplomat to the last, he did precisely the same thing with his milk. The President smiled slightly, but said nothing as he stooped down and gave his saucer to a gray cat waiting patiently at his feet.

Well, you can get in trouble if you slavishly go along with tradition without thinking first. Sometimes what seems like the proper procedure is the wrong way . . .

Profession—*Ethics*

It is awkward for me to speak tonight against my own profession. I recall a remark made by Alexander I, the liberal-minded czar of Russia. He was once approached by a man who said, "Sire, I am a republican." "So am I," replied the czar, "but my profession is against it."

And my profession, as you know, is against the stand . . .

Professional—*Career*

When the little-known rookie with the Milwaukee Braves came up for his first time at bat in a major-league game, the rival catcher said to him mockingly, "Hey, kid, you're holding your bat all wrong. You should hold it with the label up so you can read it." "I didn't come up here to read," retorted young Hank Aaron. Fifteen years later, during the 1975 season, Aaron became the all-time home-run hitter, surpassing even Babe Ruth.

Professional—*Manners*

How many times do we overhear at social gatherings lawyers and doctors being asked for their advice by people who want to take advantage of their professional expertise? William Randolph Hearst once invited Will Rogers to come to San Simeon for a weekend. Hearst had assembled a considerable company, and Rogers was the star guest whom Hearst did not fail to show off to his best advantage. A few days later Hearst received from Rogers a bill for several thousand dollars for services as a professional entertainer. He called Rogers on the phone and protested, saying, "I didn't engage you to come as an entertainer. I invited you as a guest." Rogers replied, "When people invite me as a guest, they invite Mrs. Rogers too. When they ask me to come alone, I go as a professional entertainer."

Progress—*Criticism*

We are still facing criticism but somehow it seems less strident. It has lost much of its sting. From that I infer we must be doing better. It is like the time Booth Tarkington was introduced to a fellow author. Tarkington politely inquired, "How are you?" The other, a hypochondriac, promptly proceeded to tell him. He told him for a full hour, describing in detail all of his ailments, none of which was responding to treatment.

A week later, the two met at a party. Unthinkingly, Tarkington greeted the man with the same inquiry. Again, the other regaled him with an itemization of his pathological symptoms. This time, however, he finished his recitation in fifteen minutes. Tarkington, with a glance at his watch, commented, "I'm glad to see your condition is improved."

Protocol—*Amenities*

There has been made the suggestion that we skip introducing the head table. In that regard I am reminded of what Pope Clement XIV said to his Vatican aides after his first diplomatic reception. The prelates had admonished him for returning the bows of the ambassadors. Said Clement: "I have not been pope long enough to forget my good manners."

⇊

Before the main speech there are certain amenities that must be taken care of. Some regard these as a waste of time, but I regard them as the manners and courtesies that make life easier. When Georges Clemenceau, the "Tiger of France," was attending the Versailles Peace Conference, his young aide, while traveling with him from one reception to another, complained about all the fuss of protocol. "It's nothing but a lot of hot air," grumbled the assistant as they were chauffeured in an official limousine along the Paris streets. "Young man," answered the astute premier, "all etiquette is hot air, but that's what is in our automobile tires, and see how it eases the bumps?"

Proven—*Qualifications*

In 1944 when Franklin D. Roosevelt was running against Governor Thomas Dewey for the presidency the Democrats arranged a huge Madison Square Garden rally. Among the speakers were to be Herbert Lehman, Harold Ickes, Senator Robert Wagner, father of the former Mayor of New York City, and George Jessel. Jessel felt quite humble in such company, especially speaking before some 24,000 people in a program to be broadcast across America. Although each speech had been timed before the rally, the planners simply couldn't take into account the length of the interruptions for laughter, cheering, or applause, with the result that the program was running quite long by the time Jessel was due to speak. The twelve minutes he had been allotted had been cut back to roughly a minute and a half. Jessel stood up and said, "I know Governor Dewey. He is a nice man." Suddenly an embarrassed silence swept over the restless crowd. "But then," he continued, "my Uncle Morris is a nice man too and he shouldn't be President of the United States either."

And, similarly, gentlemen, it is not a question of who is the nicer bunch of guys but who has the proven record . . .

Public Office—*Communication*

Too many public officials play roles. They either don't know or have forgotten how to relate to people on a one-to-one basis. Benjamin Disraeli once explained his success in dealing with Queen Victoria this way: "Gladstone speaks to the Queen as if she were a public department. I treat her with the knowledge she is a woman."

Public Service—*Responsibility*

In her first appearance as Queen of the Netherlands, Wilhelmina Helena Pauline Maria stood on the balcony of her palace in Amsterdam and stared with a small child's wonder at her cheering subjects. "Mama," she asked, "do all these people belong to me?"

"No, my child," replied the Queen-Regent, "it is you who belong to all these people."

Purpose—*Challenge*

Toward the end of the nineteenth century Thomas Huxley, the famous British scientist and educator, was invited to Johns Hopkins University. A student asked Dr. Huxley what he thought of the bigness of America. "I cannot say that I am in the slightest degree impressed," announced the English biologist, "by your bigness or your material resources, as such. Size is not grandeur, and territory does not make a nation. The great issue, about which hangs a true sublimity, and the terror of overhanging fate, is what are you going to do with all these things?"

And the question today is what shall we do with the challenge that has been afforded us? . . .

Purpose—*Life*

You only live when you have a purpose. I remember hearing about Paganini, who owned a wonderful Stradivarius, a violin with the power to make people laugh or cry. He willed this remarkable instrument to an Italian city, with the provision that it never be played. The violin was displayed for all to see in an exquisite case studded with diamonds. But today, all that remains of that violin is the case. The violin itself is now a small heap of dust. Wood, if used ever so slightly, remains strong, but neglected, it turns to dust.

And so it is with any institution, or especially with our own lives . . .

Purpose—*Message*

President Eisenhower never liked to give a speech without a purpose. His White House speech writer Arthur Larson used to say that in his meetings with Eisenhower to go over a speech he had drafted, the supposedly genial Ike was a sharp questioner. "Well, Arthur," the President would ask, "what's the Q.E.D.?" In Latin that stands for *quod erat demonstrandum*—that which was to be demonstrated or proved. Ike would tell Larson, "Why give a speech, if you don't want the audience to take away a specific message."

Well, what is the bottom line in what we are selling . . . ?

Purpose—*Message*

A man coming late to a session of the House of Commons met Winston Churchill, who was just leaving, and asked, "Has the Home Secretary spoken yet?" "Yes," replied Churchill, "he has been speaking for half an hour." "What is he talking about?" asked the other. "I don't know," was the reply, "he has not said yet."

Well, what is the message we want to convey . . .

Purpose—*Objective*

In his late eighties Justice Oliver Wendell Holmes was earnestly reading on a train when the conductor asked for his ticket. Frantically Holmes searched for it. "Never mind, Mr. Justice," said the conductor. "When you find it, mail it to the company." "I know I have it," exploded Holmes. "But what I want to know is where in the world I am supposed to be going."

And that is the question that confronts us today . . .

Purpose—*Youth*

Professor Mark Van Doren was lunching with some Amherst boys who asked him what they should do with their lives. "Whatever you want," said Van Doren, "just so long as you don't miss the main thing!" "What is that?" "Your own lives," said Van Doren.

We shouldn't be so wrapped up in a cause that we lose our own sense of individual purpose . . .

Qualifications—*Duty*

Two candidates applied to George Washington for a certain office. One was a dear friend, a life-long associate of Washington; the other was rather hostile to the Federalist policies of Washington —in fact, he could be found in the ranks of the opposition. Washington, to the surprise of everyone, appointed the latter to the post.

"My friend," he said, "I receive with a cordial welcome but, with all his good qualities, he is not a man of public affairs. His opponent is, with all his hostility to me. I am not George Washington, but the President of the United States. As George Washington, I would do this man any kindness in my power but, as President, I can do nothing."

But too many of us have difficulties in separating our social from our professional responsibilities . . .

Questions—*Answers*

The problem is not that we aren't being offered answers to some questions but they aren't the questions we wanted answered. When Calvin Coolidge occupied the White House, he ducked reporters so consistently that one day they formed a conspiracy against him. Before a conference to which he reluctantly had agreed, each one wrote out precisely the same question: "Are you going to run again in 1928?" Coolidge read each slip carefully, without comment or change of expression, then threw them all in the trash basket. "Gentlemen," he said, "the only question in this lot I care to answer today concerns public schools in Puerto Rico." He then delivered a fifteen-minute talk on the subject, full of statistics.

Reactionary—*Reform*

There are those who regard the most obviously needed reform as revolution—any improvement as some imperilment of the Constitution. Sir Samuel Romilly, the great legal statesman and judicial reformer, once commented on this reactionary feeling. He was shocked at the barbaric punishment for treason inherited from the Middle Ages: one guilty of high treason was to be drawn and quartered, and his bowels were to be thrown into his face while his body yet palpitated with life. When Romilly proposed abolishment in the House of Commons, the Attorney General pleaded with the House, "Are the safeguards, the ancient landmarks, the bulwarks of the Constitution, to be thus hastily removed?" Romilly replied, "What? To throw the bowels of an offender into his face, one of the safeguards of the British Constitution? I ought to confess that until this night, I was wholly ignorant of this bulwark!"

Realism—*Illusory*

The effectiveness of this so-called health plan reminds me of something Abraham Lincoln once said. On one occasion abolitionists were pressing him early in the war to free the slaves. Lincoln patiently explained that freeing the slaves in the Confederacy-held states was an empty gesture. By way of example Lincoln said, "What if I asked you how many legs has a cow?" "Four, of course," was the ready answer. "That's right," said Lincoln. "Now suppose we call the cow's tail a leg, how many legs would the cow have?" "Why, five, of course." "That's where you make an error," said Lincoln. "Simply calling a cow's tail a leg doesn't make it a leg."

And, similarly, just calling this proposal a health plan doesn't mean it is really going to provide health . . .

Reality—*Industry*

When Sir John Steell, the sculptor, had the Duke of Wellington sitting for a statue, he wanted to get him to look warlike. All his efforts were in vain, however, for Wellington was bored by such posturing. At last Sir John, his patience gone, said, "As I am going to make the statue of Your Grace, can you not tell me what you were doing before, say, the battle of Salamanca in Spain? Were you not galloping about the fields cheering on your men to deeds of courage by word and action?" "Bah!" said the duke. "If you really want to model me as I was on the morning of Salamanca, then do me crawling along a ditch on my stomach, with a telescope in my hand."

The secret of success is hard, painstaking work. It is neither glamorous nor exciting . . .

Record—*Character*

I think we can all agree how much we owe to our honoree. It can be said as a Wilmington lady once said of George Washington. This

Mrs. Rogers said it to a Colonel Tarleton of the Royal British Cavalry who had been wounded in the hand by General Washington in the Battle of Cowpens.

At a Wilmington ball the aristocratic officer spoke disparagingly of Washington: "You know actually, he's quite a country bumpkin. His mother, you know, is illiterate and I understand he can barely scrawl his own name."

"Well," replied Mrs. Rogers, "at least it can be said that he made his mark upon you."

Record—*Fame*

The man we honor tonight has built an enviable record. If he were French, he'd be given the Medal of Honor—if he were English, he'd be knighted. It's because he represents the best type of aristocracy—a meritocracy—a word which John Churchill, for one, exemplified. When Queen Anne elevated him to become the first Duke of Marlborough some members of the established nobility would not accept the newcomer because of his humble parentage. They taunted the new duke whenever the opportunity presented itself.

On one occasion, an aristocrat said mockingly, "Tell me, whose descendant are you?"

To which the Duke of Marlborough replied, "Sir, I am not a descendant, I am an ancestor."

And you can be sure that our honoree's descendants will . . .

Relaxation—*Alert*

The situation now reminds me of the time Press Secretary William Hassett was called upstairs in the White House by President Franklin Roosevelt. F.D.R. told the young aide, "Have a seat on the can but remember your pants are up."

We may be relaxing now but we can't afford to let our guard down . . .

◡

When Casey Stengel was manager of the Brooklyn team in the 1930s his squad earned the nickname of the Daffy Dodgers. One of the more "daffy" was infielder Frenchy Bordagaray. Once during a close game Frenchy squelched a Brooklyn rally by being caught off second base despite the fact he had taken hardly any lead at all. When he returned to the bench, Casey blew his top. "What happened? What happened to you—you big lug? Did you fall asleep? What happened?" "Gee, I don't know," answered Frenchy. "There I was standing on the bag tapping the base with my foot and I guess they caught me between taps."

Well, we can't afford to let our guard down even for a moment either . . .

Relief—*Replacement*

After Chaim Weizmann died, Itzhak Ben-Zvi was called to the presidency of Israel. On the day he became president, he returned home at night and found a sentry marching up and down in front of his dwelling. He asked the soldier what he was doing there. The young officer replied that he had been sent by the chief of staff to act as an honor guard before the home of the president. Ben-Zvi was truly amazed. He entered his home but in a few minutes he went out again into the cold, wintry night air. "Look here," he said to the soldier on duty, "it's cold outside. Come in and have a cup of hot tea." The soldier indicated that he could not leave his post. "Orders are orders," he informed Ben-Zvi. The president entered his home again. "Make some hot tea, please," he said to his wife. "I am going out once again to speak to the sentry." Once again he walked out and, addressing the soldier, said, "Look, I have an idea. You go in and have a cup of tea. I will stand outside with your gun and take your post."

Religion—*Faith*

Christian commitment demands not doctrinal knowledge but faith in the spiritual experience. Once Supreme Court Justice Felix Frankfurter attended a service where the Protestant theologian Reinhold Niebuhr was preaching. "I liked what you said, Reinie, and I speak as a believing nonbeliever."

"I'm glad you did," the clergyman replied, "for I spoke as a nonbelieving believer."

Religion—*Intolerant*

As a Protestant, I suppose I should feel out of place addressing a Catholic group. But I don't think it matters what church you go to, as long as you go—all churches do the work of the Lord. I recall the famous exchange between the Archbishop of Canterbury and the British head of the Catholic Church, Cardinal Hensley—in London over a century ago. Coming out of a meeting they had just attended together, the archbishop offered the cardinal a ride in his carriage. After all, said the Anglican archbishop, "We both are engaged in God's work." "Yes," the cardinal replied, "you in your way, and I in His!"

Religion—*Simplicity*

In the late 1960s Dr. Karl Barth, the eminent theologian, spoke at the Virginia Seminary. Thousands of ministers and seminarians attended to hear this seminal thinker of religious philosophy. At the end of the two-hour discourse a divinity student raised his hand and asked, "Dr. Barth, what is the most profound truth you have experienced in your lifetime?" Two, three, then five minutes passed—then Barth answered with the age-old Sunday school ditty, "Jesus loves me, this I know/ Because the Bible tells me so."

Indeed, some of our most profound truths are the simplest in expression . . .

Remembrance—*Eulogy*

When Ludwig van Beethoven died in Vienna in March 1827, his last words were these: "I close my eyes with the blessed consciousness that I have left one shining track upon the earth."

Today I want to talk about another shining track a friend of ours left on earth . . .

Replacement—*Temporary*

When William Henry Harrison died and John Tyler succeeded him as chief executive, he was the first Vice President to assume office because of the death of a President. As such he was called at first "acting President." Tyler's first act was to commission his coachman to purchase a carriage. In a few days the coachman returned and reported that he had searched Washington and had found a very handsome carriage for sale, but it had been used a few times. "That will never do," said Tyler. "It would not be proper for the President of the United States to drive around in a secondhand carriage." "And sure," said the old coachman, "but what are you, sir, but a secondhand President?"

And in a similar sense I feel my ascendancy to office has been quite circumstantial . . .

Representation—*Balance*

Senator George H. Moses came storming into the White House during the Coolidge Administration to complain that a man under consideration for a Republican senatorial nomination was "an out-and-out S.O.B." "That could be," Coolidge conceded, "but there's a lot of these in the country, and I think they are entitled to representation in the Senate."

Well, they may be entitled to representation but not to over-representation . . .

Reputation—*Name*

Our speaker today comes from a distinguished family. But no one would say of him what Alexander the Great once said of a soldier in his army who was also named Alexander. After a battle in which his namesake had fled from a skirmish, the emperor said to him, "Either change your name or live up to it."

Request—*Exhortation*

Once a patron of the British Conservative Party came to Benjamin Disraeli and asked to be appointed first lord of the admiralty.

Disraeli demurred, saying he would give him something better. "What is that?" was the response. "The chance to turn down publicly the chancellorship of the exchequer. That way you will receive all the recognition of being asked and, in addition, the superior feeling of turning it down."

In other words, people like being able to say they turned something down. It is an ego trip. For that reason you should never be afraid of asking someone—be it to head a fund drive or give a speech . . .

Rescue—*Emergency*

In military parlance "a field expedient" is an emergency measure taken even if it conflicts with rules because there is no other option. During the 1960 presidential campaign I was advancing a speech appearance by President Eisenhower. The Republican rally was held in a huge amphitheater, and just before Ike was to make his entrance, I was told that the President had to respond to a call of nature. I was asked the way to the men's room and I pointed and said that it was about seventy-five yards down that corridor and around the corner. I raced on ahead to make sure there were no hitches or obstacles. Unfortunately I found I had directed the commander-in-chief to the ladies' room. The men's room would be almost a quarter of a mile in the other direction.

Panic-stricken, I barged into the ladies' room and said, "Everybody out. Everybody out—Emergency—Everybody out." One distressed young lady washing her face cleared out without drying her face. Then I pushed the door back against the wall to hide the "Ladies" sign just before the President turned the corner of the corridor. As Ike entered, I closed the door. When I heard the flush I opened it. The President exited without any comment on the feminine dispensers.

Research—*Discussion*

Yogi Berra, hard-hitting catcher-outfielder of the New York Yankees, had a tendency to swing at the first pitch no matter where it was thrown. Yankee Manager Bucky Harris took him aside one day as he was about to go up to hit and gave him some advice. "Now look, Yogi," said Bucky, "take it easy. Don't just swing away. Try to think before you cut at the ball." Yogi took his place in the batter's box and watched three pitches sail right down the middle for strikes. As he stumbled back to the dugout, Yogi glared at Bucky. "I don't get it," he said bitterly. "How can a guy think and hit at the same time?"

Well, gentlemen, if we see a good one, we have to hit it. We can't spend all the time discussing it . . .

Respite—*Conference*

The coffee break is a fairly well-established practice. It is a term loosely used for a brief rest period whether the people stop for coffee, a soft drink, or a glass of milk. But there was one historic coffee break which stands out for two reasons. It occurred under very trying circumstances, and the man who served the coffee later became President of the United States.

On the afternoon of September 17, 1862, federal troops crossed Antietam Creek and were pressing toward Sharpsburg against fierce resistance. The sergeant in charge of the commissary department for an Ohio regiment voluntarily carried a bucket of hot coffee and a box of cooked rations to the men of his regiment along the firing line. He ladled the coffee into a tin cup and let each man have his fill. He also served the warm food from the ration box. The sergeant who instituted this historic coffee break and later became President of the United States was William McKinley. Today, a tall granite monument to the first coffee break can be seen on the site of this historic battle in western Maryland.

Now, while assuring you that I entertain no such political aspirations, I do suggest we break for coffee . . .

Responsibility—*Blame*

If there are mistakes or disasters I will assume all responsibility. In that sense I will follow Lady Peel's example. Lady Peel, known to Americans as the actress Beatrice Lillie, was in a taxi with her Pekingese dog when she saw a trickle appear on the seat. As they drew up to London's Savoy Hotel, the driver demanded: "What the devil do you mean by letting your dog do that in my taxi?" Lady Peel drew herself up. "I did it," she said, sweeping into the lobby.

Responsibility—*Credit*

As I assume this new responsibility I think of Marshal Joffre's comment after World War I. Almost everybody thought that Joffre had won the first battle of the Marne, but some refused to agree. One day a newspaperman appealed to Joffre: "Will you tell me who did win the battle of the Marne?" "I can't answer that," said the Marshal. "But I can tell you that if the battle of the Marne had been lost the blame would have been on me."

Similarly, the blame will be on me if there is a failure . . .

Responsibility—*Fate*

We don't get credit for good intentions. We get paid for results. William Lyon Phelps, teaching at Yale, found written on a pre-Christmas examination paper in English literature: "God only knows the answer to this question. Merry Christmas." Phelps returned the paper with the notation "God gets an A; you get an F. Happy New Year."

Responsibility—*Involvement*

A reporter once asked Billy Graham, "How do you explain your success?" "The only explanation I know is God." "But why," asked the journalist, "did God choose you?" "When I get to heaven," said Billy, "that's the first question I am going to ask Him."

Well, one of the first questions I'd like to ask is how did I ever come to feel so involved with . . .

Retirement—*Age*

Johnny Unitas, former professional quarterback, was once asked why he decided to stop playing football. He replied, "I could have played two or three more years. All I needed was a leg transplant."

Retirement—*Change*

When David Ben-Gurion re-emerged from retirement for the ninth time, he was asked by an American visitor why he bothered ever to resign at all. "What is the real significance behind your resigning anyway?" he asked. "Why," said Ben Gurion, "it has the same significance as those 'going out of business' signs along Seventh Avenue—a chance for one to unload some stock he doesn't want, hire new men, and make a different contract with the union."

Similarly, I regard my resignation as a chance to make some new friends, embark on some new endeavors . . .

Retirement—*Defeat*

When Winston Churchill was defeated in 1945, he was offered a dukedom by the king and the greatly coveted Order of the Garter. Said Churchill, "Why should I accept the Order of the Garter from His Majesty when the people have just given me the Order of the Boot."

And I suppose I should ask why I am being awarded this plaque in the face of my recent defeat. But then I think I am accepting this as a measure of recognition for all my friends and supporters . . .

Retirement—*Priority*

I have things to do before I retire. I think of the words of Ethan Allen whenever I am told I should take it easy. The old hero of Ticonderoga was dying. His physician leaned toward him and said, "General, I fear the angels are waiting for you." The old general replied, "Waiting, are they? Waiting, are they? Well, goddamn 'em, let 'em wait!"

Revolution—*Movement*

When the attack upon the Bastille began the night of July 14, 1789, King Louis XVI, in his isolated Versailles apartments, said, "Why, it's only a revolt." "Sire," replied the Duc de La

Rochefoucauld, "it is not a revolt, it's a revolution."

In a similar sense we can say the events we are now witnessing are no passing phases . . .

Ridicule—*Humor*

The greatest weapon is wit. No one can stand being laughed at. Nothing is more shameful to the arrogant and pompous. In the middle of the 1930s Mayor LaGuardia was faced with a very difficult problem. A high-ranking German diplomat was due for a state visit in New York. Shocked and angered by the recent anti-Jewish laws of the Nazis, a great number of New Yorkers threatened to do bodily harm to the diplomat. The mayor himself abhorred the Nazis, but it was his sworn duty to prevent violence. He solved the problem by surrounding the Nazi representative with a bodyguard of police. They all had one thing in common—they were Jewish. The joke embarrassed the Nazis and caused enormous laughter. But it also resolved a potentially dangerous situation.

And I think ridicule is the weapon we should utilize . . .

Risk—*Sacrifice*

Henry VIII appointed Sir Thomas More to carry an angry message to Francis I of France. Sir Thomas told His Majesty that if he carried such a message to so violent a king as Francis it might cost him his head. "Never fear," said Henry, "if Francis should cut off your head, I would make every Frenchman now in London a head shorter." "I am obliged to Your Majesty," said Sir Thomas, "but I much fear if any of their heads will fit my shoulders."

And like Sir Thomas I'm loyal to a point, but I'd be crazy to lend support to this proposition . . .

Role—*Parent*

Like every other President, William Howard Taft had to endure his share of abuse. One night at the dinner table his youngest boy made a disrespectful remark to him. There was a sudden hush. Taft became thoughtful. "Well," said Mrs. Taft, "aren't you going to punish him?" "If the remark was addressed to me as his father he certainly will be punished," said Taft. "However, if he addressed it to the President of the United States, that is his constitutional privilege."

Similarly, the answer to that question depends on what role I am in . . .

Sacrifice—*Commitment*

I realize in making this commitment that I am not making the sacrifices some of you others are making. Some of you, possibly, have far more to lose. It reminds me of what Samuel Chase of Maryland told Elbridge Gerry at the signing of the Declaration of Independence. Chase, a huge, beefy-faced fellow of 250 pounds, was asked by Gerry of Massachusetts why he decided to risk his property holdings in Maryland to sign the Declaration. Turning to the frail, spindly Gerry, he said, "It's you who will have the far more difficult time. With your slight build you're likely to keep dangling on the gallows, while I will only but suffer for a moment."

Sacrifice—*Exertion*

When Coach Bob Zuppke was coaching his fighting Illini some years ago, he loved to instill fighting spirit in his teams with fiery harangues before the games. With a bunch of untried sophomores, Zuppke was having a tough season when the Iowa game came along. There was little chance for Illinois to win, and Zuppke really poured it on in the dressing room before the game. "This is the supreme test, men!" he boomed to the assembled squad. "Steel yourselves for your greatest effort! Get out there and be ready to die for Illinois. There'll be no one taken out of the game unless he's dead!" Out went the raging Illini. They played themselves into the ground trying to stave off the superior Iowa eleven. Late in the game, one of the Illinois players suddenly collapsed on the field. Zuppke sprang up. "All right, you!" he snapped at a sophomore substitute. "Go out there and replace that man!" "Yes, sir," gasped the startled youth. He rushed out on the field, looked down at the stricken warrior for a moment, and then came trotting back to the sideline. "What's the matter with you?" shouted

Zuppke. "Get back there on the field and take that man's place!" "It ain't necessary, coach," answered the green sophomore timidly. "He's still breathing a little."

Well, to those of you who are half dead from the recent all-out effort, I want to . . .

Sacrifice—*Mother*

In the mid-nineteenth century a young woman made a journey one winter by foot over the mountains in north Wales to take her young baby to the nearest doctor for a checkup. Starting back in late afternoon, she ran into a blizzard on top of the mountain. She lost her way in the swirling snow as she blindly descended, half-frozen by the icy wet chill. She never made it home. She was found the next day dead—frozen to death curled around her young baby. But the baby was still alive. The mother's warmth had saved the baby boy. Because of that mother's sacrifice the world was to have the leadership of her son, David Lloyd George.

Sacrifice—*Unambiguous*

Charles Carroll of Maryland did not have to vote on the Declaration of Independence. Yet he insisted on signing after the fact. He journeyed to Philadelphia in August 1776 to pen his name. When the millionaire planter did sign, John Hancock, president of Congress, said, "There goes two million up in smoke." Carroll's answer was to sign unambiguously, "Charles Carroll of Carrollton" so that the British would surely know of his sentiments for independence.

Well, it's time for some of you to stand up and be counted in an unambiguous and clear way . . .

Sample—*Disapproval*

I have seen enough to know I don't like it. In that way I am like former Ambassador Walter Hines Page, who was also a distinguished New York editor. Like other editors, he was obliged to refuse a great many manuscripts. A lady once wrote him, "Sir, you sent back last week's story of mine. I know that you did not read the story, for as a test I had pasted together pages 18, 19, and 20, and the story came back with these pages still stuck together, and so I know you are a fraud and turn down stories without even reading them." To which Mr. Page replied, "Madam, at breakfast when I open an egg I don't have to eat the whole egg to discover it is bad."

Satisfaction—*Intemperate*

One night in the privacy of the Oval Office, John Kennedy was asked how come he called the big steelmen who had raised their prices S.O.B.s. Wasn't that kind of angry candor a luxury that Presidents could not allow themselves? "Yes," said Kennedy, getting that faraway look. "It was not very wise. But it felt so good."

Well, in a similar way, I can say my comments were not very wise . . .

Science—*Reactionary*

The most implacable opponent of the Truman Administration in the Senate was Robert Taft. Taft at the time served as a trustee of Yale along with Truman's Secretary of State, Dean Acheson. At one Yale meeting Taft arrived after discussion had already begun and asked Acheson what the subject was. Acheson replied that it was the condition of study and research in the natural sciences at Yale, which, it seemed, required improvement. At that point, without a moment's hesitation, Taft interrupted the speaker by announcing: "Mr. President, I went through Yale without taking a single course in science." While the Yale Corporation was recovering in complete silence from this remarkable revelation, Dean Acheson addressed the president of the university, saying, "Your Honor, the prosecution rests." The silence was broken.

Self-Importance—*Perspective*

A newly appointed bishop, received by Pope John XXIII in a private audience, complained that the burden of his new office prevented him from sleeping. "Oh," said John kindly, "the very same thing happened to me in the first few weeks of my pontificate, but then one day my guardian angel appeared to me in a daydream and whispered, 'Giovanni, don't take yourself so seriously, try laughing at yourself,' and ever since then I've been able to sleep."

Self-Interest—*Motive*

A great philosopher once put his finger on man's greatest inducement. Lord John Russell said to David Hume, the Scottish philosopher: "What do you consider the object of legislation?" "The greatest good to the greatest number." "What do you consider the greatest number?" "Number one," replied Hume.

Sensationalism—*Journalism*

In the Spanish-American War of 1898, James Gordon Bennett of the New York *Herald* was upset at his Havana correspondent's routine coverage of the war. He wired to the reporter this advice: "Don't let yourself be inhibited by the facts."

Well, in the recent publicity the press has followed Bennett's advice . . .

Sense—*Beauty*

Helen Keller once wrote a letter to John Greenleaf Whittier complimenting him upon his poetry: "It is very pleasant to live here in our beautiful world. I cannot see the lovely things with my eyes, but my mind can see them all, and so I am joyful all the day long."

In our case, however, our eyes as well as our minds can enjoy the beauty of this work . . .

Sensitivity—*Communication*

Jed Harris, the stubborn producer of *Our Town,* and other plays became convinced he was losing his hearing. He went to a specialist who gave him a thorough checkup. The doctor pulled out a gold timepiece and asked, "Can you hear this ticking?" "Of course," said Harris. The specialist walked to the door and held up the watch again. "Now can you hear it?" Harris concentrated and said, "Yes, I can hear it clearly." The doctor walked out the door into the next room and said, "Can you hear it now?" "Yes." "Mr. Harris," the doctor said, "there is nothing wrong with your hearing. You just don't listen."

The problem in most failures of communication is that we fail to listen. We are thinking of what we are going to say when we should be concentrating on what the other person has to say . . .

Sensitivity—*Responsiveness*

If I had to list the most essential quality for a leader in my field I would have to agree with former university president James B. Angell. At a dinner in his honor, Doctor Angell, who for thirty-eight years was president of the University of Michigan, was asked by a reporter, "President Angell, what is the secret to lasting so long as a president of a big university?" Dr. Angell replied, "Grow antennae, not horns."

In other words, one must be aware and sensitive to developing trends and currents . . .

Service—*Commitment*

We honor today a man who has never sought praise or honor. One might say that he followed the advice given to that veteran lawmaker of the twentieth-century Carl Hayden. After being sworn in in 1913 Hayden was taken aside by Congressman Joshua Talbott of Maryland. Talbott told the young Arizonan, "There are two kinds of Congressmen, show horses and work horses. If you want to get your name in the paper, be a show horse. If you want to gain the respect of your colleagues, keep quiet and be a work horse."

Service—*Humanity*

Thousands of appeals for pardon came to President Abraham Lincoln from soldiers involved in military discipline cases. Each appeal was, as a rule, supported by letters from influential people. One day a single sheet came before him, an appeal from a soldier without any supporting documents. "What!" exclaimed the President. "Has this man no friends?" "No, sir, not one," said the adjutant. "Then," said Lincoln, "I will be his friend."

Today each of us has the chance to be a friend . . .

Service—*Patriotism*

We should not be ashamed of our patriotic feelings. Benjamin Disraeli wasn't. In August of 1865, when Mr. and Mrs. Disraeli paid a visit to Raby Castle, home of the Duke and Duchess of Cleveland, the future Prime Minister, Lord Rosebery, was charmed by the brilliant leader of the Conservative Party.

After the Disraelis left, Rosebery looked into the visitors' book where the names of guests and their professions were recorded. It said: B. Disraeli, Profession: Patriotism.

Service—*Public Interest*

During a series of congressional investigations into a highly suspicious series of land sales, a Boston lawyer, Louis Brandeis, later a Justice of the Supreme Court, appeared before the committee as a representative of a group of citizens alarmed at the waste in the public interest. When Brandeis took the witness stand, a Congressman challenged his right to be present. "Who, sir," he asked, "do you represent?" "I, sir," replied Brandeis, "represent the people. The public is my client."

It is my hope and belief that this new officer of the government will also be the people's counsel and speak for the people . . .

Settlement—*Compromise*

Fortunately, in our discussions we were dealing with reasonable men who did not close their ears to constructive comment. In that regard I had a better experience than David Lloyd George. When he was questioned on some of the provisions of the Versailles peace treaty after World War I he replied, "Well, it was the best I could do, seated as I was between one who thought he was Jesus Christ and the other who thought he was Napoleon Bonaparte."

Silence—*Discretion*

When some newspapermen asked Cardinal Francis Spellman a great many questions during a surprise interview, he pointed to a mounted fish on the wall behind his desk which had an interesting label attached. It read, "If I had kept my mouth shut, I wouldn't be here."

Similarly, I don't plan to respond to a lot of iffy questions . . .

Similarity—*Language*

He may be a Republican but he sounds like a Democrat. I am reminded of an observation made by Abraham Lincoln. Once on an eight-mile ride to a corps review, six mules pulled the President's vehicle over a rough corduroy road that jolted the passengers. All the while the driver let fly volleys of oaths at the mules. Lincoln leaned forward, touched the driver on the shoulder, and said, "Excuse me, my friend, are you an Episcopalian?" The surprised driver looked around. "No, Mr. President, I am a Methodist." "Well, I thought you must be an Episcopalian because you swear just like Governor Seward, who is a church warden." The driver, by the way, stopped swearing.

Sincerity—*Belief*

Jean Baptiste Massillon, the great orator of the pulpit, was once asked by Louis XIV which were his favorite sermons. Father Massillon replied, "The ones I know best in my own heart."

Skeptic—*Change*

Sometimes the skeptics just don't want to be convinced. I recall the story of the gala crowd that had assembled for the test run of Robert Fulton's outlandish steamboat contraption, the *Clermont.* For some hours, in the presence of a mass of spectators, the strange craft belched smoke and sparks from its tall, thin stack as its engineers attempted to get up the necessary head of steam. When the time to cast off came and the engines were being limbered up, the boat quivered and vibrated violently and made a loud racket. A group of doubting Thomases in the crowd had been shouting loudly and scornfully, "She'll never start! She'll never start!" But despite the skepticism the boat pulled itself together and actually started to move up the river. After a moment of astonished silence, the voices of the scoffers resumed their shouts

—this time crying with all the scorn they could muster, "She'll never stop! She'll never stop!"

Smallness—*Greatness*

Dr. Oliver Wendell Holmes was a rather small man, but there was nothing diminutive about his spirit. Once when he was present at a gathering of unusually tall men he was asked, as a joke, if he did not feel somewhat small and insignificant in the company of such big, strapping fellows. "Indeed I do," replied Dr. Holmes tartly. "I feel like a dime among a collection of pennies."

Well, looking at the head table, I feel like a penny next to a lot of dimes . . .

Socialism—*Business*

It is cheap demagoguery to rail at millionaires. The truth is that even if you confiscated all the millionaires' holdings, it would be a minuscule amount of revenue compared to what an additional one percent tax on those making over $15,000 would come to. Economists, however, oppose crushing taxation on the grounds it would slow down the economy and depress incentive.

Andrew Carnegie was once visited by a socialist who preached to him eloquently the injustice of one man's possessing so much money. He preached a more equitable distribution of wealth. Carnegie cut the matter short by asking his secretary for an assessment of his many possessions and holdings, at the same time looking up the figures on world population in his almanac. He figured for a moment on his desk pad and then instructed his secretary, "Give this gentleman sixteen cents. That's his share of my wealth."

Soldier—*Professional*

During the War of 1812 General William Henry Harrison interrupted a difficult expedition when one of his soldiers, laboring under the hardship of the march, died. A Christian funeral and burial were ordered. As General Harrison paused to watch the building of the coffin, one of the soldiers weary of the long campaign approached Harrison, thinking it was an opportune time, to ask, "General, is the army going to continue this expedition?" Harrison looked at him and said, "Are you a soldier, sir?" "Yes." "Then, sir, be one."

Similarly, we must continue to act as professionals . . .

Solution—*Exit*

P. T. Barnum solved the problem of overcrowding in his popular New York museum where customers were apt to stay too long by rigging up a corridor wall leading toward the doorway to the street and displaying above it prominently the sign TO THE EGRESS.

Well, I wish we could find such an easy out to our predicament . . .

Speaker—*Advocate*

When President Franklin D. Roosevelt was a young lawyer just getting started in New York he was retained to handle a difficult civil case. The opposing lawyer was a very effective jury pleader and completely outshone his youthful rival in the argument to the jury. However, he made one fatal mistake: he orated for several hours. As he thundered on, Roosevelt noticed that the jury wasn't paying much attention. So, playing a hunch when his turn came, he rose and said: "Gentlemen, you have heard the evidence. You also have listened to my distinguished colleague, a brilliant orator. If you believe him, and disbelieve the evidence, you will have to decide in his favor. That's all I have to say." The jury was out only five minutes and brought in a verdict for Roosevelt's client.

Now, you have been bombarded in the press by a lot of rhetoric, but I would like you to remember these few facts . . .

Speaker—*Talents*

Once when Orson Welles was lecturing in a small Midwestern town before a very sparse audience, he opened his remarks with a brief sketch of his career. Said he, "I'm a director of plays and also a producer of plays. I am an actor of the stage and motion pictures. I write and produce motion pictures and I write, direct, and act on the radio. I'm a magician and painter. I've published books. I play the violin and the piano." At this point he paused and, surveying his audience, remarked, "Isn't it a pity there's so many of me and so few of you!"

Like Orson Welles, a speaker is also many persons but fortunately our audience has more than a few . . .

Speaker—*Welcome*
In 1860 Senator William Henry Seward and Senator James Nye, in company with Charles Francis Adams, visited the town of St. Anthony, Minnesota. A welcoming committee awaited the party of dignitaries at the station, but unfortunately the group came by a different route. At the dinner a lawyer who had the responsibility of introducing Seward said in his remarks, "Mr. Seward, we are sorry, indeed, that we did not have the opportunity of escorting you into town, but we assure you that we shall take greater pleasure in escorting you out of it."

Similarly, though our arrangements today became somewhat fouled up, I assure you we will take great pleasure . . .

Speech—*Acceptance*
People ask why I travel and give so many speeches. Well, in that respect I compare myself to Warren Harding. The father of the President once told him: "Warren, if you were a girl, you'd be in a family way all the time—you can't say no."

Speech—*Audience*
Mrs. Vanderbilt once demanded to know what Fritz Kreisler would charge to play at a private musicale, and was taken aback when he named a price of five thousand dollars. She agreed reluctantly but added, "Please remember that I do not expect you to mingle with the guests." "In that case, madam," Kreisler assured her, "my fee will be only two thousand."

Well, I can assure you, contrary to Fritz Kreisler's fee demands, that if I had known all these nice people were going to be here, I would have spoken free . . .

Speech—*Organization*

When Mark Twain was lecturing around the country, he once found himself in a small Pennsylvania town and went to the local barbershop to freshen up before the evening appearance.

"You are a stranger in town, sir?" asked the barber.

"Yes, I'm a stranger here," was the reply.

"We're having a good lecture tonight sir," said the barber, "a 'Mark Twain' lecture. Are you going to it?"

"Yes, I think I will," said Samuel Clemens.

"Have you got your ticket yet?" the barber asked.

"No, not yet," said the other.

"Then, sir, you'll have to stand."

"Dear me!" Mr. Clemens complained. "It seems as if I always have to stand when that fellow Twain talks."

Well, I assure you I'd much rather be sitting in the audience and hear one of the several outstanding members of your group talk.

Speech—*Preparation*

Former Supreme Court Justice Felix Frankfurter was late for dinner one night at the home of a Harvard faculty colleague. Finally, he sent his cab driver to the door to convey this apology: "Professor Frankfurter asked me to tell you that he will be in in about ten minutes. He is still in the taxi. He has not yet arranged his conversation for the evening."

The point is that even the greats prepare ahead their bon mots for the evening's conversation . . .

Speech—*Silence*

A newly elected Member of Parliament went to Prime Minister Disraeli for advice. "For the first six months," Disraeli told him, "you should only listen and not become involved in debate." "But my colleagues will wonder why I do not speak!" protested the other. Said Disraeli, "Better they should wonder why you do not, than why you do!"

With that advice I will refrain at this time from talking and pass
to someone else . . .

Speech—*Spokesman*

When Winston Churchill celebrated his eightieth birthday in November 1954 the prime minister was honored in Westminster Hall
by lords and commons. "I have never accepted," he said modestly,
"what many people have kindly said, namely that I inspired the
nation. Their will was resolute and remorseless, and, as it proved,
unconquerable. It fell to me to express it and if I found the right
words you must remember that I have always earned my living by
my pen and by my tongue. It was the nation and the race dwelling
all around the globe that had the lion's heart . . . but I had the luck
to be called on to give the r-o-a-r."

Although I have few qualities of a Churchill, I have been made
the spokesman . . .

Speech—*Toastmaster*

Jean Baptiste Massillon, a celebrated member of the French
clergy, was once told by King Louis XIV, "Father, I have heard
many great orators, and I have been satisfied by them, but when
I hear you, I am dissatisfied with myself."

As chairman of tonight's dinner and as an occasional speaker, I
want to say that if you make me dissatisfied with myself, you have
left the audience more than well satisfied by your eloquent presentation.

Spending—*Cost*

I am getting a little worried about the mounting costs of this
project. In that sense I feel like the writer Irvin Cobb. In World
War I, Cobb served as a correspondent and was sent to Belgium
when the Germans invaded that country. He and three other
newsmen engaged a taxicab to drive them to the Belgian army
headquarters. They ran into the advancing Germans and were
taken prisoner. After a night spent under guard, the four were
questioned by an officer. The interrogation lasted for hours. A full

day had passed since their capture, and still the officer kept hammering at them with his questions. Cobb became increasingly fretful. Finally he could no longer contain himself. "Sir," he called out, his nervousness apparent, "whether or not you intend to shoot us, will you at least grant us one request?" "What is that?" said the German. "Will you please," begged Cobb, "tell the driver of our taxicab to stop the meter?"

Spokesman—*Speech*

As a young army officer in 1906 Douglas MacArthur was assigned as an aide-de-camp to President Theodore Roosevelt. MacArthur was a great admirer of the President and often had the opportunity to talk with him. One day he asked Roosevelt what he felt to be the single factor accounting for his popularity with the masses. "To put into words," the President replied, "what is in their hearts and minds, but not their mouths."

Sport—*Alumni*

In dealing with alumni I sometimes feel not unlike Indiana basketball coach Bobby Knight. After Indiana was beaten by Purdue and the alumni had called for his scalp, Knight told his assistant coach, "I think all alumni should be canonized. That way, coaches would only have to kiss their rings."

Sport—*Golf*

Benjamin Rush commented in 1775 on the British game called golf, which was still largely unknown in America. "There is a large common in which there are several little holes," Rush explained. "The game is played with little leather balls stuffed with feathers and sticks made somewhat in the form of a bandy-wicket and he who puts a ball into a given number of holes with the fewest strokes gets the game." When an American asked what the game was good for, Rush said, "A man who plays golf, it is said, will live ten years longer."

Sport—*Message*

When Johnny Sain, the great National League pitcher, was a young rookie with the Braves he faced the fabulous Rogers Hornsby for the first time. Sain said, "I knew he was the greatest hitter of all time, but I figured I could fool him by pitching carefully."

Johnny threw one ball that didn't quite catch the corner of the plate. He threw another, which also missed, according to Umpire Bill Klem. Johnny was getting annoyed, and when Umpire Klem called the next close pitch a ball, Sain walked halfway to the plate and said sarcastically, "Say, Ump, will you let me know when I pitch a strike?" "Young man," replied Umpire Klem, "when you pitch a strike, Mr. Hornsby will let you know."

And, similarly, our speaker is a man whose very accomplishments send a message . . .

Standards—*Excellence*

When the celebrated bon vivant of the Roman world General Lucullus was eating alone one evening, he noted that the table had only moderate provisions and expressed his dissatisfaction. The servant explained that he thought that since the general had no guests he would not want an expensive feast. "What?" said Lucullus. "Did you not know that this evening Lucullus sups with Lucullus?"

Well, even when we have no one to please but ourselves, we have our own inner standards. We know when we have done our very best . . .

Statistics—*Facts*

One afternoon in the House of Commons, Prime Minister Churchill was asked by a member of the Labor opposition for some potentially embarrassing statistics bearing on some of the Churchill government's programs. Churchill replied, "I will have an answer for tomorrow's session." The next day, true to his word, he rattled off figures for the better part of an hour. Later, his secretary, amazed, asked, "How could you compile those statistics in a single day? It would have taken me and my staff six months to get them for you." "Right," agreed Churchill, "and by the same token, it will take the opposition six months to prove I am in error."

Success—*Ambition*

When Andrew Jackson was President, Davy Crockett presented himself at the White House with a number of his followers. The head usher called out, "Make room for Colonel Crockett, make room for Colonel Crockett." The backwoodsman snorted and said, "Colonel Crockett makes room for himself," and he strode into the White House hall.

And, similarly, our speaker has had no one preparing the way. He did what he did on his own . . .

Success—*Humor*

Senator Tom Corwin of Ohio once gave this advice to a young aspiring politician: "Never make people laugh. If you would succeed in life you must be solemn, solemn as an ass. All the great monuments are built over solemn asses."

Fortunately, our speaker is a living proof that belies such advice. He is both humorous and successful . . .

Success—*Negotiation*

I learned the secret of negotiation from Arthur Goldberg. When he was Secretary of Labor President John F. Kennedy called him in after a labor strike had been averted and said, "How do you do it, Arthur?" Goldberg said, "The trick is to be there when it's settled."

Successor—*Wishes*

After some years of marriage the wife of novelist John O'Hara divorced him. Writers were too temperamental and unpredictable, she complained, and she no longer could put up with this one's quirks and peccadilloes. What did she do next, however, but fall in love with still another famous author. O'Hara read of the wedding and sent his former bride this cable: "Heartiest congratulations and best wishes. (signed) Frying Pan."

So as another frying pan I want to . . .

Suicide—*Anticlimactic*

Billy Rose was a great impresario. One day a forlorn individual came to him with this startling proposition: "I'll do an act in your show that will be the greatest sensation ever presented. You can advertise it in advance, and get $100 a ticket. If you'll put $25,000 in escrow for my wife, I'll then commit suicide in the full view of your audience." "It's a natural!" said Rose, simulating enthusiasm, "but just a minute. What will you do for an encore?"

And I think anything I would say after the gentleman's self-inflicted injuries resulting from his own statement would be . . .

Supplies—*Harassment*

In 1863 General Stonewall Jackson received a dispatch from the Confederacy's Secretary of War Judah Benjamin asking detailed questions. Jackson wired back, "Send me more men and fewer questions."

I understand how Stonewall felt. Right now I would do better if I had some more resources and had to face fewer questions . . .

Support—*Forgiveness*

As I come before you today, I feel that perhaps I should ask your forgiveness in the same way Frank Clement once did. The thirty-four-year-old Tennessee Governor was once asked in public such an embarrassing question about his personal life that, although he was an experienced and fluent speaker, it nearly got the best of him. He had a well-deserved reputation as a bon vivant, gourmet, and all-around playboy, and one night a few of his chickens returned to roost.

He was addressing a church group and, in spite of being a bit overstimulated, he made a brilliant speech. Questions followed, which he handled with ease and skill, until a woman stood up and, fixing Clement with a piercing eye, said sternly, "Governor, I have heard that you drink too much and are too fond of women, and I just want to know—is this true?" There was a gasp from the audience at the frankness of the question. Then all eyes sought the governor's face. There was complete silence in the hall for several seconds. When he finally broke it, it was to say, looking sincerely at the questioner, "Sister, pray for me!"

Support—*Partisanship*

Lord Melbourne, British Prime Minister, once stormed into a London newspaper office and berated the editor for not giving him sufficient support. "I always support your party when you are right," said the editor in his own defense. "We don't want your support when we are right," said Melbourne indignantly. "What we want is a little support when we are in the wrong."

Such are the demands and dangers of party loyalty . . .

Target—*Criticism*

King Frederick William II of Prussia, was a big man—tall and broad. It is said that, in battle, the eighteenth-century king would ride through the ranks urging the soldiers to a forward charge. "Look," he would say, "which of you offers so large a target?"

Well, neither am I afraid to be a target for criticism if that is the cost for spearheading a cause . . .

Teacher—*Education*

The author and historian Thomas Carlyle once received a letter from a young man which read as follows: "Mr. Carlyle, I wish to be a teacher. Will you tell me the secret of successful teaching?" Carlyle immediately wrote back, "Be what you would have your pupils be. All other teaching is unblessed mockery and apery."

Timidity—*Conference*

When writer Eugene Field was dramatic critic on the Denver *Post,* he was asked to review a performance of Shakespeare's *King Lear.* His review was terse but pointed: "Last night at the Tabor

Opera House, a man who purported to be an actor played the King. He played it as though under the premonition that someone was to play the Ace."

Well, selling is the same way. You can't act as if someone is always going to say no . . .

Timing—*Age*
Somerset Maugham, the famous writer, recuperating in London from a bout with the flu, was phoned by a female admirer. "Could I send you fruit," she asked, "or would you rather have flowers?" Replied the eighty-eight-year-old Maugham, "It's too late for fruit —too early for flowers."

Timing in any offer is of the essence . . .

Timing—*Scheduling*
On the TV program "Double or Nothing" I once heard Bert Parks ask a young couple, "How long have you two been married?" "Eight years," replied the husband. "Eight and a half," corrected the wife. "What difference does half a year make?" Parks teased. "Well," retorted the wife, "we have a little girl seven and a half."

And, similarly, timing does make a difference. As I look at the schedule for the next year . . .

Timing—*Strategy*
Once when Casey Stengel was managing the Brooklyn Dodgers, he lifted his pitcher in the fourth inning for a pinch hitter. Trailing the Cardinals by three runs, the Dodgers had a real opportunity with the bases loaded. His hitter, Babe Phelps, smacked a home run for four tallies. Though the Dodgers went ahead they later lost their lead. In the ninth, one run behind, there was need for another pinch hitter. One of the grandstand experts called out to Casey, "Yah bum, yah," he yelled. "Why did you waste Phelps before—now's when ya really need him."

And in this sales campaign we have to decide when is the best time to really unload our big guns . . .

Togetherness—*Team*

During World War II Jimmy Durante was doing a tour of veterans' hospitals under the supervision of Ed Sullivan. At one rehabilitation center on Long Island, Sullivan warned his friend, "Look, Jimmy, no encores—we have a tight schedule. Our plane leaves at eleven-fifteen sharp." Well, when the time came, there was the great Schnozzola doing an encore. From behind the curtain Sullivan motioned to Durante. Durante went over to Ed and said, "Look, Ed, plane or no plane, I can't leave—look at the pair of soldiers clapping in the second row." They were one-armed veterans clapping together with their good arms.

So whatever our handicaps, if we join our talents and work together . . .

Traitor—*Defection*

When Senator Wayne Morse of Oregon switched from the Republican to the Democratic Party in 1956, Ambassador Clare Boothe Luce commented to a reporter's question this way: "Remember, whenever a Republican leaves one side of the aisle and goes to the other, it raises the intelligence quotient of both parties."

Travel—*Authority*

Though I have never been there, that still does not exclude me from any expertise. The late Arthur Waley, the British scholar of Chinese and Japanese antiquities, finished in 1932 a translation of *The Tale of Genji* which remains an elegant classic. It has influenced many who have studied Japan and its culture in any way, shape, or form. But Waley never visited Japan. Admiral Yamamoto Isoroku, while serving as naval attaché in London, once asked Waley how many times he had gone there. "Never," his reply is reported to have been. "I have no intention of going to Japan. That would spoil it."

Truth—*Falsity*

We are constantly told to accept the assurances on faith. But our faith is wearing a little thin. I am reminded of the late Clarence

Darrow, who once defended an author in one of those trumped-up plagiarism cases and had occasion to challenge the veracity of a dubious witness. "But," protested the witness, "I am wedded to the truth." "Oh," nodded Darrow, "and how long have you been a widower?"

Truth—*Statesmanship*

A newspaperman once asked Sam Rayburn, "Mr. Speaker, you see at least a hundred people a day. You tell each one yes or no. You never seem to make notes on what you have told them, but I have never heard of your forgetting anything you have promised them. What is your secret?" Rayburn's brown eyes flashed. "If you tell the truth the first time," he replied, "you don't have to remember."

Undertaking—*Completion*

When the Spanish conquistador Hernando Cortez began his conquest of Mexico, he ordered his ships to be burned on the Gulf of Mexico shore in full view of his men so that they all might feel that there was no hope for them except in victory.

Well, in a similar sense, there can be no turning back for us . . .

Unearned—*Appointment*

As everyone knows, I owe my appointment to certain political powers that be. In that sense I can agree with Leo Durocher. Durocher was known as the expert needler and bench jockey when he was a manager in the major leagues. Once when the New York Giants were playing an exhibition game at West Point, the Cadets were giving the needle to Leo, asking how a runt like him ever made it to the big leagues. Leo's answer was classic: "I got appointed by my Congressman."

Similarly, I got appointed . . .

Unenthusiastic—*Recommendation*

I do not wish to criticize. I am sure the gentleman has many supporters. But my reaction is a lot like that of Abraham Lincoln when he was called upon at the White House and asked to give an endorsement to a book. He told the author to leave the book with him and he would see what he could do. Later, the author returned to find this recommendation: "For people who like that kind of a book, that is the kind of a book they will like."

Unfair—*Retaliation*

Once Cornelius Vanderbilt wrote the following letter to certain business rivals: "Gentlemen: You have undertaken to cheat me. I will not sue you, for law takes too long. I will ruin you. Sincerely yours, Cornelius Vanderbilt."

Well, if this practice continues we will sue and get even too . . .

Unintelligible—*Mediocrity*

I know the economic situation is pretty complicated. But just because we don't completely understand doesn't mean we can't assess the effectiveness of present policies. I recall once when the musician Otto Klemperer was conducting a modern work that he hated. In the middle of the performance some boy in the audience got up and walked out, whereupon Klemperer turned around and said, "Thank God somebody understands this piece of work."

Unique—*Best*

John Ringling North, the young head of Ringling Brothers Barnum and Bailey, once called upon the city editor of the St. Louis *Post-Dispatch*. At the city desk he announced, "Hurray and Happy Tidings! The circus is in town." The editor scowled and said, "What circus?" North threw his hands in the air. "What circus? When they say the band is playing 'God Save the King' do you ask what king?"

And, similarly, when we say the clinic in Rochester we don't say what clinic . . .

University—*Education*

As an educator I try to make few promises. One, however, I will hold myself to is what Woodrow Wilson said to a parent when he was president of Princeton University. An anxious mother was questioning him closely about what Princeton could do for her son. "Madam," the exasperated Wilson finally replied, "we guarantee satisfaction or you will get your son back."

University—*Priority*

When Woodrow Wilson was at Princeton, where he was a popular teacher and later president, he cracked down on students who were not attending school for an education. One boy was expelled for cheating. His mother made a trip to Princeton to talk with Wilson. She had a sad tale of personal sickness and worry, and she pleaded with Wilson to reinstate her boy because of the possible adverse reaction it would have on her. Wilson heard the woman's plea. "Madam," he began, "you force me to say a hard thing. If I had to choose between your life or my life or anybody's life and the good of this college, I should choose the good of the college."

Well, the good name of the institution is what we are concerned about today . . .

Unoriginal—*Copy*

Once during a joint appearance by Fred Allen and Jack Benny, the sometime violinist got off a jibe at Allen's expense. Whereupon Fred replied, "That was a very funny remark, Jack. Your writers did very well—but the fact is you couldn't ad-lib a belch after a Hungarian dinner."

Unusual—*Unique*

Just before the turn of the century there was a crisis at the Barnum and Bailey Circus. The man who was shot out of the cannon every day was asked by his wife to quit his high-risk job. The great P. T. Barnum, whose wit was equal to his showmanship, called him and said, "I beg you to reconsider—men of your caliber are hard to find."

Well, men of the caliber of our speaker are hard to find too—and he is also in a high-risk profession . . .

Unworthy—*Criticism*

Sam Houston while president of the Republic of Texas received a challenge to fight a duel from a person he considered his inferior. Turning to the bearer of the challenge, he said, "Sir, tell your principal that Sam Houston never fights downhill."

And in the same way I am not going to respond . . .

Urban Problem—*Conspicuous*

That celebrated landmark of Paris, the Eiffel Tower, has been the topic of much conversation over the years. In the nineteenth century, William Morris, the English poet, during a long stay in Paris very nearly cloistered himself in the restaurants of the Eiffel Tower, not only taking all his meals but even doing much of his writing there. "You're certainly impressed by the tower," someone once remarked to him. "Impressed," said Morris. "I stay here because it's the only place in Paris where I can avoid seeing the damn thing!"

And, similarly, there are few places I can go where I can avoid seeing the blight and rot of urban decay . . .

Urgency—*Humanity*

We should recall the words of the great French general, Marshal Lyautey, who once asked his gardener to plant a certain kind of tree. The gardener demurred, saying, "Marshal, this tree is slow growing and will not reach maturity for a hundred years." Lyautey replied, "In that case, we have no time to lose—plant it this afternoon."

Today, a world of knowledge, a world of plenty, a world of peace may be years away. But we have no time to lose. Let us plant our trees this afternoon . . .

Values—*Responsibility*

When Wall Street financier Bernard Baruch made his first million, he went to tell his father about it. His father, however, did not seem to be impressed. "I am not even thirty," said Bernard, "and already I have made my first million—and you are not even happy?" "No, my son," replied his father, "I am not impressed. What I want to know is—how will you spend the money you have earned?"

What are the values we are teaching our children? . . .

Verbosity—*Impractical*

The overblown language of bureaucrats once prompted former British Prime Minister Benjamin Disraeli to comment on the oratory of William Gladstone. Gladstone, who had the air of a man who had just descended from Mt. Sinai with the tablets, was once answered thus by Disraeli after a particularly grandiloquent speech: "My right honorable opponent is a rhetorician inebriated by the exuberance of his own verbosity."

And I think our friends, too, have let themselves be a bit carried away by the grandness of their proposal . . .

Viewpoint—*Narrow-mindedness*

One of the basic elements in British Prime Minister David Lloyd George's domestic policy was Home Rule. The prime minister considered that every one of the four countries of the United Kingdom should have local autonomy, subject only to the overriding authority of an Imperial Parliament. Lloyd George's "Federal Solution" was the subject of some heckling at one of his campaign stops. "Home Rule for Ireland! Home Rule for Wales! Home Rule for Scotland! Yes, and Home Rule for England, too," declaimed the orator. "Home Rule for Hell!" interrupted a heckler. "Quite right," said Lloyd George, "let every man speak up for his own country."

And the criticism from certain quarters would seem to indicate they almost want hell or, at least, have no hope of salvation . . .

Visit—*Sights*

Samuel Johnson was once taken by his friend James Boswell to see the Great Causeway in Ireland. He arrived at the site in a disagreeable mood, having been brought there on horseback, a method of conveyance he thoroughly despised. He shrugged his shoulders contemptuously as he gazed at the columnar basalt rock, which is considered one of the wonders of the world. "Isn't this worth seeing?" Boswell asked him. "Yes," replied Johnson, "worth seeing. But not worth going to see."

Well, I cannot say this has been my experience in the visit to your city . . .

Woman—*Accomplishments*

Once a lady approached Senator Henry Clay, saying, "You do not remember my name?" "No," was the prompt and gallant response, "for when we met long ago I was sure your beauty and accomplishments would very soon compel you to change it."

Well, the accomplishments as well as the beauty of the speaker are distinctive, for everyone is aware of the impact she has had . . .

Women—*Clubs*

I assure you I have a high esteem for this organization. Clubs like yours contribute to the strength and character of a community. I certainly don't agree with W. C. Fields. Once Fields was asked to speak at a society's annual banquet. He gruffly demurred. "But surely you believe in clubs for women?" said the matron. "Certainly," said Fields, "but only if all other means of persuasion fail."

Women—*Feminists*

We have indeed come a long way since the days of Samuel Johnson. Dr. Johnson was once in conversation with a very forthright lady, of whom he appeared to take very little notice. "Why, Doctor, I believe you prefer the company of men to that of the ladies," she accused him. "Madam," replied he, "I am very fond of the company of ladies; I like their beauty, I like their delicacy, I like their vivacity, and I like their silence."

Well, here is one woman who won't hesitate to speak out . . .

Women—*Lineage*

Once the beautiful and accomplished niece of the British minister to America engaged President Andrew Jackson in a conversation. To the general, who was the victor of New Orleans in 1814, she said, "Mr. President, you and General Washington enjoy a unique fame. No one else has ever defeated my countrymen." "That, my dear lady," replied Old Hickory, "is because both of us were descended from your countrywomen."

And I am proud to say that my mother was a member of your organization . . .

Women—*Vanity*

Male chauvinists considered women drivers a traffic problem in the narrow, twisted streets of Paris even in the pre-revolutionary days of King Louis XVI. It was the custom for society ladies of the time to chauffeur their own carriages, and not even the king dared risk their displeasure by forbidding them to drive. Summoning one of his shrewdest ministers, Count d'Argenson, the king asked him whether he could diplomatically unsnarl the traffic jams. "Of course," said d'Argenson. "I will simply promulgate this law: Ladies under thirty years of age are forbidden to drive carriages."

Work—*Dedication*

Shortly after he opened his first plant, Thomas Edison noticed that his employees were in the habit of watching the lone factory clock. To the inventor, who was an indefatigable worker, this was incomprehensible. He did not indicate his disapproval verbally. Instead, he had dozens of clocks placed around the plant, no two keeping the same time. From then on, clock watching led to so much confusion that nobody cared what time it was.

That's the way work should be—not a time-card-punching operation . . .

Writer—*Retired*

Now that I am working at home I find some of the domestic help looking at me somewhat strangely. I remember once when Mrs. William Dean Howells, wife of the noted American novelist, had hired a girl to do the housework. Several weeks passed and, seeing Mr. Howells constantly about the house, the girl formed an erroneous impression. "Excuse me, Mrs. Howells," she said one day, "but I would like to say something." "Well, Kathleen?" The girl blushed and fumbled with her apron. "Well, you pay me five dollars a week—" "I really can't pay you any more," interrupted Mrs. Howells apologetically. "It's not that," hastily answered the girl, "but I am willing to take four till Mr. Howells lands a job."

Subject Index

Name Index